AM

Mata Amritanandamayi

AMMA'S PEARLS
OF WISDOM

Publication compiled by
Valérie Servant

Translated from Malayalam by
Embracing the World

Published in India in 2018 by Harper Element
An imprint of HarperCollins *Publishers*
A-75, Sector 57, Noida, Uttar Pradesh 201301, India
www.harpercollins.co.in

2 4 6 8 10 9 7 5 3 1

PISBN: 978-93-5277-373-2
EISBN: 978-93-5277-374-9

The views and opinions expressed in this book are the author's
own and the facts are as reported by her, and the publishers are
not in any way liable for the same.

Mata Amritanandamayi asserts the moral right
to be identified as the author of this work.

This book was originally published in French as
Tout est en vous. Paroles d'Amma, by Editions Points

The excerpts proposed in this book were selected by
Valérie Servant from the speeches and words of Mata
Amritanandamayi, known as Amma, as transcribed and
translated by the members of Embracing the World, Amma's
network. The titles of the texts were chosen by Valérie Servan

Typeset in 10.5/14 Janson Text LT Std
by Jojy Philip, New Delhi 110 015

Printed and bound at
Thomson Press (India) Ltd

Where love is present, there is no effort
The happiness of others is my respite

Amma

CONTENTS

AMMA: LOVE IN ACTION

⊷ ✺ ⊷

'My religion is love'
Amma

Mata Amritanandamayi is regarded as one of the great spiritual figures of our time. More universally known as Amma – 'mother' in Malayalam, the official language spoken in Kerala – she declares that her religion is love. In India, she is considered to be a 'Mahatma', or a Great Soul.

Amma is the incarnation of love, truth, renunciation and self-sacrifice in the very noblest sense. She does not stop at teaching; she puts her teachings into practice every second, every day of her life. Established in plenitude, she gives everything. This is why we feel the divine in her presence.

Even though she never married, nor had children, she has become the mother of all. Considered by thousands as the Mother of Compassion, she is both a great master and a universal mother.

To those who tend to hide away from others, or cut themselves off from their immediate surroundings, Amma shows the way of giving and opening the heart. She teaches the path of unity and infinite compassion.

Her famous darshan, the embrace that bestows, in her own words, 'an uninterrupted flow of love', is a simple yet powerful gesture. This gesture of unconditional love has become the symbol of her international reach. Since 1975, she has taken into her maternal arms, one by one, more than thirty-four million people across the globe, touching the hearts of all who come to her.

However, it doesn't end with the darshan, because Amma is 'compassion in action'; through her organization Embracing the World, she comes to the aid of the world's poorest and most destitute.

Amma's life is her only message: Give everything, give of yourself.

A SHORT BIOGRAPHY

Amma was born on 27 July 1953 into a family of humble fishermen on the Kerala coast, southern India. She was one of thirteen children. As early as five, Amma showed extraordinary mystical qualities. She was consumed with love for the divine, and she already wrote and sang devotional songs.

Amma was only nine years old when her mother

fell ill. The whole responsibility for the household fell on her shoulders. She was obliged to leave school, but she offered her long hours of work to the Lord.

At the age of thirteen, she experienced her first rapture. After rigorous and austere spiritual practices, she increasingly went into samadhi (a deep meditative state), and stayed like this for hours on end, sometimes even for days, without showing any signs of consciousness.

At the same period, the girl felt a profound call to serve the poor, to whom she gave much care and attention. She stole butter and milk from her parents and gave them to those in need. She tried to comfort people both materially and physically by holding them in her arms. A spontaneous attitude which may seem natural, but which, at the time, was considered to bring shame on her family: young Indian women were not allowed to touch other people, let alone men, not to mention people belonging to a different caste.

As a teenager, her trances became more frequent. Members of her own family and villagers simply could not fathom her; she did not behave like a 'normal' young woman. But no one could stop her from her mission.

By the age of twenty, this young woman's aura was already considerable: people came from further and further away to meet her, and a community of disciples grew. Gradually, she came to be honoured for the extraordinary qualities that emanated from her. For those close to her, she is the feminine incarnation of the divine.

In 1975, at the age of twenty-two, she left the family home and was forced to live outside. The fact that the sky was her only roof, the earth her bed, the moon her lamplight, and the sea breeze her fan has become a legend. The birds and the other animals kept her company and became her faithful companions. They brought her food and served it to her.

It was at this time that Amma asserted her true mission: to relieve the world's suffering and guide the steps of spiritual seekers. Ever since, inexhaustibly, in forty countries, on all five continents, she has continued embracing and serving. Her darshan inspires many people to volunteer and to serve those who suffer in life.

In 1981, her ashram was built at her birthplace. In 1987, at the age of thirty-four, she made her first world tour. Today, her time is divided between her main ashram in India and the tours she makes every year to the United States, Europe, Japan and other parts of India, where she meets disciples, followers and the simply curious who come to experience her darshan. Everywhere in the world, communities have been founded around her message: 'To give love and compassion to the poor and suffering is our duty towards God.'

HUMANITARIAN ACTION

Amma is not only about darshan. She was presented with the Gandhi-King Award for peace and non-violence for her internationally renowned charitable work.

Thanks to donations gathered from across the globe, Embracing the World's scope of action equals that of a state. This NGO is an international network of charitable works supporting women, children, orphans, the poor, and victims of natural disasters.

A tsunami in Indonesia, India or Sri Lanka, the nuclear accident in Fukushima, an earthquake in Nepal? Amma's volunteers rally immediately to help, in love and selfless service. Embracing the World has given more than fifty-one million euros in emergency aid since 1998.

The NGO has developed multiple actions including food distribution (ten million meals served to the homeless and starving in India; every year, 75,000 people receive support in the United States in forty-one towns), free housing (45,000 houses built for the homeless in India), pensions for widows, orphanages, education, vocational training, and health care (free health care delivered to three million patients, hospitals, etc.). It has also developed five university campuses, which have already become references in the field of computing and research over just a few years.

These are just some of the actions so far accomplished. As for the future as many projects are already in the pipeline.

Anne Ducrocq
June 2015

'In today's world, there are two types of poverty: the first is due to a lack of food, clothing or housing, and the second is due to a lack of love and compassion. We must first deal with the second type of poverty because if our hearts are full of love and compassion, we will give our heartfelt service to all those who have no food, no clothes and no shelter.'

Amma

NOTE: THE NOTION OF GOD

The word *God* is used for convenience. In the tradition into which Amma was born, this world is the manifestation in infinite forms of a singular 'energy' of love and light. This is the One God, the Divinity, the Divine Mother. It points to that unfathomable mystery of supreme Consciousness, the Absolute, the All, Emptiness, unconditional Love, Peace that surpasses all understanding, abiding Joy, etc.

This energy of love and light is our true nature. The *Self*. The divine within.

It is the *mind* that prevents access to it, hiding our true nature with its conditioning, beliefs, fears and desires.

Brahmacharini Dipamrita (Claudine Tourdes),
Amma's representative in France

JANUARY

January 1 – *Living with joy*

Not just one day, but all three hundred and sixty five days of the year should be filled with joy. Our entire lives should become a festival! Spirituality teaches us the way to accomplish this. For this surrender to take place, total refuge in the Supreme Being is required.

January 2 – *The yoga of writing*

It is a good habit to write a diary every day, preferably before going to bed. In your diary you can note down how much time you have devoted to your spiritual practice each day. Write the diary in such a way that it helps you see your mistakes. Then, make the effort not to repeat them. Your diary should not merely be a document of other people's faults or your daily transactions.

JANUARY 3 – *Stop the pendulum of the mind*

The mind can be compared to a pendulum. Like the incessant movement of a clock's pendulum, the pendulum of the mind swings back and forth from happiness to sorrow. When the pendulum of the clock moves to one extreme, it is only gaining enough momentum to swing back to the other end. Likewise, when the pendulum of the mind moves towards happiness, it is only gaining the momentum to reach the other pole of sorrow. Real peace and happiness can be experienced only when the pendulum of the mind stops swinging altogether. From that stillness, real peace and bliss ensue. This state of perfect stillness is verily the essence of life.

JANUARY 4 – *Reaching out*

To consider someone unworthy of the spiritual path is like deciding, after building a hospital, that no patients are allowed. Even a broken watch will show the correct time twice a day! So, what is needed is acceptance. When we avoid someone as 'unsuitable', we are helping to engender vengefulness in that person, and he or she will again slip into error. On the other hand, if we praise what is good in such people and try patiently to correct their mistakes, we can uplift them.

JANUARY 5 - *God is present in everything*

God is present everywhere: in the singing cuckoo bird, the cawing crow, the roaring lion, and the thundering ocean. It is that same Power that sees through our eyes, hears through our ears, tastes through our tongue, smells through our nose, feels through our skin, and powers our legs as we walk. It is this Power that fills everything. It must be experienced.

JANUARY 6 - *May we become insatiable seekers*

Today, we search outwardly for the causes and solutions to all the problems of the world. In our haste, we forget the greatest truth of all, which is that the source of all problems is to be found in the human mind. We forget that the world can become good only if the mind of the individual becomes good. So, along with the understanding of the outer world, it is essential that we also get to know the inner world.

JANUARY 7 - *A single right action is enough*

If a person does a hundred good things and makes just one mistake, people will despise him and reject him. But if a person makes a hundred mistakes and does just one good thing, God will love him and accept him. Be therefore bound only to God, my children. Dedicate everything to Him.

JANUARY 8 – *Strengthen our minds*

Set aside some time each day for reading spiritual books. Have a book on your master's teachings or a book like the Bhagavadgita, the Ramayana, the Bible, or the Koran available for daily reading. Memorize at least one verse a day. You should also read other spiritual books when you have time. Reading the biographies and teachings of the great masters will help strengthen your spirit of renunciation and help you easily understand the spiritual principles.

JANUARY 9 – *Surrender*

My children, we should surrender our minds to God. This is not easy because the mind is not an object we can just pick up and give away. However, when we surrender something the mind is attached to, it is the same as surrendering the mind. When we give up the wealth to which our minds are attached, we are actually surrendering our minds. Only the prayers flowing from a heart that has developed this attitude of surrender will bear fruit. God has no need for our wealth or prestige. The sun doesn't need the light of a candle. Our worldly wealth will definitely vanish sooner or later. But if we install God in its place, we become the owners of everlasting joy.

JANUARY 10 – *Make a vow of non-violence*

Non-violence should be the vow of our lives. To practise non-violence is to refrain from hurting any creature in the slightest way through thought, word or deed.

JANUARY 11 – *Developing our consciousness*

We have a tendency to feel proud of our knowledge. But if we stop for a moment to think about it, we will realize that we are leading an almost unconscious life. How many times a day are we really aware of our own body? When we eat, we are neither aware of our own hands that feed us, nor of the tongue inside our mouth. When we walk, we are unaware of our own legs. Are we conscious of our breathing? As we look around and observe all the beauty and ugliness before us, are we aware of our own eyes? We are leading an unconscious life.

JANUARY 12 – *Expect nothing*

My children, always act without expecting the fruits of your actions. Expectation is the cause of all suffering.

JANUARY 13 – *Keeping our eyes wide open*

To show compassion towards suffering humanity is our obligation to God. Our spiritual quest should begin with selfless service to the world. People will be disappointed if they sit in meditation, expecting a third eye to open after closing the other two. This is not going to happen. We cannot close our eyes to the world in the name of spirituality and expect to evolve. To behold unity while viewing the world through open eyes is Spiritual Realization.

JANUARY 14 – *Balancing the material and the spiritual*

As our awareness of the goal grows stronger, our attachments to material pleasures drop away naturally. Giving up pleasures is not as important as cultivating the right attitude towards those pleasures. Only when the spiritual and material aspects of life are in balance, like the two wings of a bird, can there be harmony in society.

JANUARY 15 – *A world free of all selfishness*

My children, no one loves anyone more than they love themselves. Behind everyone's love is a selfish search for their own happiness. When we don't get the happiness we expect from a friend, our friend becomes our enemy. This is what can be seen in the world. Only God loves us selflessly. And it is only through loving Him that we can love and serve others selflessly. Only God's world is free from selfishness. We should focus all our love and attachment on Him alone. Then we won't despair if we are abandoned or wronged by anyone.

JANUARY 16 – *Immutable truth*

Humanity doesn't need a new truth. What is required is to see the already existing Truth. There is only one Truth. That Truth always shines within all of us. That one and only Truth can neither be new nor can it be old. It is always the same, unchangeable, ever new. Asking for a new Truth is like a pre-primary pupil asking his teacher: 'Miss, you have been telling us that 2+2 is 4 for such a long time. It has become so old. Why can't you say something new, like that it is 5 instead of 4 all the time?'

Truth cannot be changed. It has always been there and has always been the same.

JANUARY 17 – *Unity and love*

We need to see and understand the inside, the essence of religion, from a spiritual perspective. Only then will rivalry between different religions come to an end. Where there is division, there cannot be any spiritual experience; and where there is true spiritual experience, there will be no division – only unity and love.

JANUARY 18 – *Complementarity*

There is a man in the inner depths of every woman, and a woman in the inner depths of every man. This truth dawned in the meditation of the great saints and seers eons ago. This is what the half-God and half-Goddess concept in the Hindu faith signifies. Whether you are a woman or a man, your real humanity will come to light only when the masculine and feminine qualities within you are balanced.

JANUARY 19 – *Life cannot be blamed*

You complain that you can't take one more step in the sun, because you are too exhausted from the heat. Yet, all the while you have been carrying an umbrella under your arm! That is your condition now: if you had only unfolded your umbrella and held it over you, the sun wouldn't have made you tired. Spiritual power and spiritual qualities exist within you, but because you are not aware of them, you experience sorrow. Life cannot be blamed for this. All you need to do is get rid of the ego and install God in its place. There is no need to go anywhere in search of peace. Truth and noble ideals – that is God. But there is no room for such ideals in a mind filled with the sense of 'I'. The ego should be eradicated with the help of humbleness. Then, through the power within us, we will experience peace. By heating metal in a fire, we can mould it into any shape we like. Similarly, by offering our ego to the fire of God, we can transform ourselves into our true nature.

JANUARY 20 – *We are One*

There is no difference between the Creator and creation. They are essentially one and the same: Pure Consciousness. We should learn to love everyone equally, because in essence we are all one; we are all One soul. Though outwardly everything appears different, inwardly we are all manifestations of the Absolute Self.

God is the Pure Consciousness that dwells within everything. We need to understand this truth, and thereby learn to accept and love everyone equally.

JANUARY 21 – *All paths lead to the same goal*

People belong to different cultures and have different tastes. The spiritual masters have indicated different paths to suit different tastes. Even though the paths may appear to be different, their essence is the same and they all lead to the same goal.

JANUARY 22 – *The realm of the spirit*

The mind that has had a real taste of even a little bit of spirituality cannot find happiness in worldly things. If a man marries someone other than the girl he loves, he'll be unhappy with his wife, because his mind will be on the one he loves. Similarly, the mind that has turned to spirituality can no longer find satisfaction in the material realm.

JANUARY 23 – *Placing our trust in wisdom*

You can't see the current in a live wire. Do you say there is no current, just because you cannot see it? You'll get a shock if you touch it. That is experience. Suppose you set a bird free to fly away. It flies higher and higher, until it finally soars to such a height that it can no longer be seen. Do we say that the bird no longer exists because we cannot see it? What logic is there in deciding we will believe only in that which falls within the limited range of our eyesight? For a judge, the statements of a thousand people who say they didn't see a crime being committed do not prove a thing. The proof lies with the one person who says he or she witnessed the crime. Similarly, whoever says there is no God doesn't prove anything; the proof lies in the words of the holy sages who have experienced God.

JANUARY 24 – *In the depths of the ocean, there are no waves*

It is natural that desires and emotions arise in the mind, but some restraint is necessary. It is natural to feel hungry, but we don't eat whenever we catch sight of something edible. If we did, we would get sick. Likewise, the craving for excessive pleasures leads to suffering. People don't realize that the pleasure they receive from the senses really comes from inside themselves. They chase frantically after external happiness until they collapse in a state of suffering and despair. Then, again they run around and again they collapse. If you go in search of external pleasures only, you won't find peace in life. You have to learn to look inward, for that is where real bliss is to be found. But you won't find that bliss until your mind's outward leaps are stopped and the mind becomes still. In the depths of the ocean there are no waves. Similarly, you will find that the mind automatically becomes still as you enter into the depths of your mind. Then there is only bliss.

JANUARY 25 – Inner change

Only an inner change based on a spiritual outlook will bring peace and put an end to suffering. Most people are adamant in their attitudes. Their slogan is: 'Only if you change, will I change.' This won't help anyone. If you change first, the other person will automatically change as well.

JANUARY 26 – Your divine beloved

The form becomes clear only when you develop pure love for the deity. As long as you cannot see God, you should be feeling a relentless sense of anguish.

A disciple should have the same attitude towards God as a lover towards his beloved. His love should be such that he cannot bear being separated from God, not even for a moment. If a lover last saw his beloved dressed in blue, then, whenever he sees just a hint of blue anywhere, he sees his beloved and is reminded of her form. While eating and even in his sleep, his mind rests only on her. When he gets up in the morning and brushes his teeth and drinks his coffee, he wonders what she is doing at that moment.

This is the kind of love we should have for our Beloved Deity. We shouldn't be able to think about anything else but our object of worship.

JANUARY 27 – *Doing one's duty*

There was once a spiritual master who had a disciple in the army. War broke out with another country. The disciple had never fought in a war. Having heard many terrible war stories, he was scared at the very mention of the word *war*. He ran away from the army and went to his master. He told the master that he no longer wanted to do any work and wished to become a monk. The master knew that his disciple wanted to become a renunciate only out of fear and not out of any true detachment. He therefore instilled the disciple with courage and sent him back to the battleground. The master didn't do this because he himself had any interest in war; but at that particular time it was the duty of his disciple to fight because he was a soldier.

It is never right to be a coward and run away; nor can a person who lacks courage ever attain liberation by taking the vows of a monk. The master taught the disciple about his proper duty and gave him the strength to carry it out. Would it be right to tell a soldier on the battlefield to give up everything and become a monk because that is the path to liberation?

Soldiers have the responsibility of safeguarding the security of their country. If they fail to carry out their duty, they betray both themselves and the country. When a country's safety is at stake, the role of a soldier is not to leave the world and become a renunciate, but to fight the enemy. If the soldier at that time decides to renounce everything, he won't succeed – Nature won't permit it.

JANUARY 28 – *Channel your thoughts*

By pasting a three-word poster on a wall saying 'Stick no bills', we can avoid hundreds of words. It is true that our notice itself is a poster, but it serves a larger purpose. Chanting a mantra is similar. By chanting a mantra, we reduce the number of thoughts. When other thoughts are kept away, the tension that normally arises from those thoughts is removed. At least while chanting, the mind is calm; there is no anger or negativity. The mind is purified. Selfishness decreases and we gain expansiveness of mind. We also create good vibrations in Nature.

If the water that flows through many different channels is directed into one channel, we can use it to produce electric power. Through mantra repetition and meditation, we can control the power of the mind, which is otherwise lost in a multitude of thoughts. In this way, we can conserve and build up our energy.

January 29 – *A helping hand*

We are seldom willing to reach out to ordinary people. We don't find the time to share their sorrows. We are not ready to offer them whatever assistance we can. But, in fact, doing so is also a way of worshiping God. If only we were willing to do this, we would secure the key that opens the door to the world of joy.

January 30 – *Spend time alone to grow stronger*

We have to prepare the field before we sow the seeds. We have to get rid of the weeds, plough the earth, make it smooth and even, and then, finally, we can plant. And as the crop begins to grow, we have to keep removing the weeds. But later, when the plants are fully grown, we no longer have to worry about the weeds, because then the plants will be strong enough to resist and the weeds cannot harm them.

In the beginning, however, when the plants are young and fragile the weeds can easily destroy them.

So in the beginning we should do our spiritual practices in solitude. We should immerse ourselves in prayer and meditation, without mingling too much with others. Our field should be free from obstructing weeds. At a later stage, when we have been doing spiritual practice for some time, we'll have the strength to transcend all external obstacles.

JANUARY 31 – *God's visible form*

By looking at Nature and observing its selfless way of giving, we can become aware of our own limitations. Thus, Nature helps us to become closer to God and teaches us to truly worship Him. In reality, Nature is nothing but God's visible form which we can behold and experience through our senses. Indeed, by loving and serving Nature, we are worshiping God Himself.

FEBRUARY

FEBRUARY 1 – *Asserting our values*

The foundation of all values is spirituality. If we lose our values, our lives become like a satellite that has broken free from the earth's gravitational pull.

FEBRUARY 2 – *Our power is infinite*

When a child is born, he or she is not conditioned by anything. But the people who surround the child – his parents, siblings, friends and society – teach him to acquire different habits. They raise him in a certain way, in a certain culture, with its own language, food, education, religion, customs and habits. Everything around him conditions him. We teach him everything – except about the infinite power of his own Self.

FEBRUARY 3 – *Develop the art of listening*

There are four ways of communicating effectively with others: reading, writing, speaking and listening. We have been well trained to read, write and speak from our childhood, but our listening skills are not as well developed as the other three. This is why most people do not know how to listen. God gave us two ears and just one mouth. We should listen twice as much as we speak, but generally, it is the opposite that happens: we speak a lot but do not listen correctly. We must develop the art of listening. If we can listen, we will gain many benefits in our lives, and be better able to make others happy. This art will help us act appropriately in all situations and will avoid frequent troubles.

FEBRUARY 4 – *Responsibility*

The biggest mistake is to do what is wrong even though you know what is right.

FEBRUARY 5 – *Disciples of love*

Love is our true essence; love has no limitations of religion, race, nationality or caste. We are all beads strung on the same thread of love. To awaken this unity and to spread the love that is our inherent nature to others is indeed the true aim of human life.

FEBRUARY 6 – *'Home at last'*

Life should be like a pleasure trip. When we see a beautiful sight, a pretty house, or a flower on the way, we look at it and enjoy it. We enjoy the sights but we do not linger there; we simply move on. When it's time to return, no matter how beautiful the things around us are, we leave them behind and go home, because there is nothing more important to us than getting back home. Similarly, in whatever manner we live in this world, we shouldn't forget our real home to which we must return – we should never forget our goal. No matter how many beautiful sights we may see on our way through life, there is only one place that we can call our own, where we can rest, and that is our point of origin – the Self.

FEBRUARY 7 – *Offerings*

If you perform your actions as offerings to God, you can transcend destiny.

FEBRUARY 8 – *A compassionate heart*

Some people believe that God is someone sitting somewhere up in the sky. They spend money lavishly to please God. But God's grace cannot be obtained just by spending money. Serving the poor is dearer to God than anything. God is far more pleased when He sees a poor person being helped and comforted, than when millions are spent on an ostentatious religious festival. God's grace pours forth when He sees you wiping the tears of a suffering soul. Wherever God beholds such a pure mind, there He hastens to dwell. A compassionate heart is a far more precious dwelling place to God than any silken couch or golden throne.

FEBRUARY 9 – *Experience true Love*

There is love and Love. You love your family, but you do not love your neighbour. You love your son or daughter, but you do not love all children. You love your father and mother, but you do not love everyone the way you love your father and mother. You love your religion, but you do not love all religions. You may even dislike those of other faiths. Likewise, you have love for your country, but you do not love all countries, and may feel animosity towards different people. Hence, this is not true Love; it is only limited love. The transformation of this limited love into Divine Love is the goal of spirituality. In the fullness of Love blossoms the beautiful, fragrant flower of compassion.

FEBRUARY 10 – *Reconnect with Nature in childlike innocence*

The one factor which connects a human being to Nature is the innate innocence within man. When we see a rainbow, or the waves of the ocean, do we still feel the innocent joy of a child? An adult who experiences a rainbow as being nothing but light waves will not know the joy and wonder of a child who sees a rainbow, or a child who is watching the waves of the ocean.

Faith in God is the best way to sustain this childlike innocence in man. He who has faith and devotion to God, which in turn stems from his innate innocence, beholds God in everything, in every tree and animal, in every aspect of Nature. This attitude enables him to live in perfect harmony, in tune with Nature. The never-ending stream of love that flows from a true believer towards the entire Creation will have a gentle, soothing effect on Nature. This love is the best protection of Nature.

It is when our selfishness increases that we begin to lose our innocence. When this happens, man becomes estranged from Nature and begins to exploit her. Man doesn't know what a terrible threat he has become to her. By harming Nature, he is paving the way for his own destruction.

FEBRUARY 11 – 'I choose my path'

If you dig a well on top of a mountain, you may not find water, even if you dig hundreds of feet. But if you dig only a small hole next to a river, you will soon find water. In the same way, your close proximity to a true master will quickly bring out your good qualities, and your spiritual practices will soon bear fruit. Now you are the slave of your senses, but if you live in accordance with the Master's will, the senses will become your slaves.

February 12 – *Charity feeds the soul*

Try to spend at least an hour each day doing some service for others. Just as the food we eat nurtures the body, doing selfless service nurtures the soul. If you don't have enough time to do this every day, set aside at least a few hours per week for acts of altruism and generosity.

February 13 – *Opening up to God's grace*

The sun shines its light everywhere. We need only open the doors and windows to experience it. Similarly, God is constantly bestowing His grace upon us, but we have to open the doors of our hearts to receive that grace. God is infinitely compassionate. It is our own mind that lacks compassion towards us, and acts as an obstacle, hindering us from receiving God's grace.

February 14 – *Universal mother*

Anyone – woman or man – who has the courage to overcome the limitations of the mind can attain the state of universal motherhood. The love of awakened motherhood is a love and compassion felt not only towards one's own children, but towards all people, animals and plants, rocks and rivers – a love extended to all of nature, all beings. This love, this motherhood, is Divine Love, – and that is God.

FEBRUARY 15 – *Discover the unknowable*

Science, which so far has developed through the human intellect, can only be perfected through meditation. Only through the knowledge of the inner Self can science reach its highest peak. As far as modern science is concerned, the entire world falls in two categories: the known and the unknown. But it is the unknowable, that which is far beyond the intellect, that we must seek to discover. That is God, or our own Self.

FEBRUARY 16 – *Striving for lasting peace*

The leaders of three religions – A, B and C – once decided to convene a meeting to bring about peace. God was so pleased with them that he sent an angel to them during the meeting. The angel asked the leaders what they wished. The leader of religion A said, 'Religion B is responsible for all the problems. So please, wipe it from the face of the earth!' The leader of religion B said, 'Religion A is the cause of

all our troubles. You have to reduce them to ashes!'
By now, the angel was disappointed. The angel
turned expectantly to the leader of religion C. With
an expression of grave humility, C's leader said, 'I
wish nothing for myself. It will be enough if you
merely grant the prayers of my two colleagues!'

This story is a parody of contemporary efforts
towards peace. Even as people smile at one another,
hatred and distrust boil within. Peace is essential to
all of us. But peace is not just the absence of war and
conflict; it goes well beyond that; it is the spirit of
harmony within ourselves. Peace should be fostered
within the individual, within the family and within
society. Simply transferring the world's nuclear
weapons into in a museum will not in itself bring
about world peace. The nuclear weapons of the mind
must first be eliminated. This is the role of religions.

Only those who experience true peace within
themselves can give peace to others. Until we rid
ourselves of our own hatred and hostility, all our
attempts to achieve everlasting peace are bound
to fail; for our attempts will be tainted by our
individual likes and dislikes.

FEBRUARY 17 – *The body is merely an instrument of the Self*

When we stop fanning ourselves with a hand-held
fan, the flow of air stops, but this doesn't mean that

there's no air. Or when a balloon bursts, it doesn't mean that the air which was in the balloon ceases to exist. It is still there. In the same way, the Self is everywhere. God is everywhere. Death occurs, not because of the absence of the Self, but because of the destruction of the instrument known as the body.

FEBRUARY 18 – *The miracle of the present moment*

My children, even if you lose a million dollars, it can be recovered. But if you lose one second, you cannot get it back. Every moment in which you are not remembering God is lost to you.

FEBRUARY 19 – *Becoming pure*

Even if we chant our mantra a million times and go on countless pilgrimages, we won't attain God if we harbour ill will towards others or trample them underfoot. The only result of milk poured into an unwashed pot is that the milk will be spoiled. Good actions purify the mind.

FEBRUARY 20 – *Living at last!*

Spiritual life is like standing in the middle of a fire without getting burned.

FEBRUARY 21 – *Experience is the way*

Religion is not limited to the words of the scriptures. It is a way of life. Its beauty and charm are expressed in the love and compassion of those who live in accordance with its precepts. Whatever Amma has said until now is like the script on the label of a medicine bottle. Simply reading the label will not effect a cure. The medicine has to be taken. You cannot taste the sweetness of honey by licking a piece of paper on which the word *honey* has been written. Likewise, the principles described in the religious texts must be contemplated, meditated upon, and finally realized.

FEBRUARY 22 – *Sharpening our discernment*

Meditation and spirituality are inseparable aspects of life. A meditative mind and spiritual thinking are essential if we want clarity and subtlety in our thoughts and actions. To see spirituality and life as separate is sheer ignorance. Just as food and sleep are necessary for the body, spiritual thinking is necessary for a healthy mind.

FEBRUARY 23 – *Cultivate good thoughts*

Attachment and aversion are not things that we can just pick up and discard. The bubbles in the water will break if we try to pick them up. We can't catch them. In the same way, it's not possible to just throw our thoughts and emotions out of our minds. If we try to suppress them, they'll grow twice as strong and create difficulties. It is only through contemplation that we can eliminate our negative emotions. We should examine our own negative tendencies and weaken them through good thoughts. They can't be eliminated by force. If we pour fresh water into a tumbler of salt water, and continue to pour even after it is full, the saltiness will decrease, and finally we'll end up with a glass full of fresh water. Similarly, we can eliminate bad thoughts only by filling the mind with good thoughts.

FEBRUARY 24 – *Acceptance is freedom*

If you are born in a body, you are bound to experience both happiness and sorrow, for that is the nature of life. Happiness and sorrow interchange according to your actions. Coolness is the nature of water and heat the nature of fire. It is the nature of a river to flow. The river keeps flowing; it doesn't stop permanently anywhere. If you understand this, you can cheerfully accept both pleasure and suffering when they come your way. Those who do this are not affected by any of the obstacles that arise from this world. They are always blissful. That is liberation.

FEBRUARY 25 – *Living your faith*

Spirituality is the cement that fortifies the edifice of society. Practising religion and living without assimilating spirituality are like constructing a tower by simply piling up bricks without ever using cement. When the wind blows even slightly, it will crumble. Religious faith without spirituality becomes lifeless, like a part of the body cut off from the flow of circulation.

FEBRUARY 26 – *Advancing side by side*

For those who have realized God, there is no difference between male and female. The realized ones have equal vision. If anywhere in the world, there exist rules that prevent women from enjoying their rightful freedom, rules that obstruct their progress in society, then those are not God's commandments, but are born out of the selfishness of men.

Which eye is more important, the left or the right? Both are equally important. It is the same with the status of men and women in society. Both should be aware of their unique responsibility, or dharma. Only in this way, can we maintain the harmony of the world. When men and women become powers that complement each other, and move together with cooperation and mutual respect, they will attain perfection.

FEBRUARY 27 – *Seeing beyond rituals and traditions*

The goal of all religions is one – purification of the human mind. To overcome our selfishness, to love and serve our fellow beings, to rise to the level of universal consciousness – these goals are common to all religions. The core of religion is to foster these human values and awaken the innate divinity in people.

Though the founders of all religions realized and practised the noblest ideals in their lives, their followers have often failed to live up to those ideals. Instead of focusing on the essence of the religious principles, love and compassion, we focus on the external rituals and traditions which vary from religion to religion. That is how these religions, which were originally meant to foster peace and a sense of unity among us, became instrumental in spreading war and conflict. This doesn't negate the importance of religious discipline and traditions. Indeed, they have their own significance. They are necessary for our spiritual development. But, we must remember that those traditions are the means to the goal, and not the goal itself.

FEBRUARY 28 – *Become a flute in the hands of the Lord*

The ego is the only thing we ourselves have created, and that is what has to be renounced. We have to surrender the ego to God. When we surrender the ego, only that which God has created remains. We then become a flute at His lips, or the sound of His conch. To rise to the level of expansiveness, all we need to do is get rid of the individual mind, which is our own creation. Once 'I' and 'mine' are given up, there is no limited individual; there is only That which pervades everything.

FEBRUARY 29 – *Hurry back to God*

If you think you will begin to keep your mind on God when all your difficulties are over and your mind has become peaceful, you are mistaken, because that is never going to happen. You will never reach God that way. It's useless to wait for inner peace.

Perseverance is the only way to better yourself. At any moment you may lose your health or mental abilities, and then your life will have been wasted. So let us follow the path to God right now. This is what is needed.

MARCH

MARCH 1 – *A mind as vast as the sky*

Once, when a truck was passing through a village, its engine somehow caught fire. The driver quickly jumped out, went to a telephone booth and called the fire department. However, by the time the fire department arrived, the front of the truck was completely burned. When the firemen opened the truck, they were surprised to see its cargo: a shipment of fire extinguishers! If the truck driver had known what was inside his truck, this calamity could have been averted.

In the same way, due to our fear, we often fail to realize the latent power within us. Fear causes our minds to shrink and shrivel. Our mind becomes like a dried-up well. Fear confines our world to a small cell of darkness, like that of a turtle that has withdrawn into its shell upon seeing a predator. We lose our power of Self. On the other hand, a fearless mind is as vast as the sky.

MARCH 2 – *Mother Nature*

Nature is our first mother. She nurtures us throughout our lives. Our birth mother may allow us to sit on her lap for a couple of years, but Mother Nature patiently bears our weight our entire life. She sings us asleep, feeds us and caresses us. Just as a child feels obligated to his birth mother, we should all feel an obligation and responsibility towards Mother Nature. If we forget this responsibility, it's equal to forgetting our own Self. If we forget Nature, we will cease to exist, for to do so is to walk towards death.

MARCH 3 – *Grounded in pure love*

In worldly life, women and men have their own needs and rights while vying to gain money, position, prestige and freedom. Striving hard to gain all these, they are expending so much time and effort. Amidst all this exertion, we should set aside a corner of our mind to remember one truth: without love, we will not be able to derive happiness or satisfaction from any name, fame, position or money. Our mind, intellect and body need to be resolutely fixed on pure love, which is the centre point of life. It is vital to work from this centre of pure love.

March 4 – *True laughter comes from the heart*

Life should blossom into total laughter. This is religion. This is spirituality. This is real prayer. God is the innocent, spontaneous smile that blossoms from within. This is the greatest prize we can give the world.

March 5 – *The virtues of repeating the divine name*

Even though we are one with the Creator, at present our minds are not under our control and so we are not aware of that oneness. We need to take control of the mind in the same way as we use the remote control of a television set to select a desired channel. Today our minds are running after many different things. Chanting the divine name is an easy way to bring back the wayward mind and to make it focus on God.

March 6 – *Cultivate humility*

Hardly anyone wishes to be humble. People don't have any humility because they are proud of what isn't real. The body is a form filled with nothing but ego, the sense of 'I'. The body is polluted by the ego and by anger and desires. To be purified, you need to cultivate such qualities as humility and modesty. By perpetuating the ego, your pride in the body increases.

For the ego to be eliminated, you have to be willing to have the attitude of humbleness and of bowing down to others.

MARCH 7 – *All names are His*

By whatever name you call it, the Divine Power is one and the same. People cherish different pictures of God in their hearts. They know God by different names, but the all-pervading Consciousness is beyond all names. God is not someone who responds only if He hears the sound of a certain call – He dwells in our hearts, and He knows our hearts. God has an infinite number of names. Every name is His.

MARCH 8 – *Fruitful discipline*

Progress is not possible without discipline. A nation, institution, family or individual can advance only by heeding the words of those who deserve respect, and by obeying the appropriate rules and regulations. My children, obedience is not a weakness. Obedience and humility lead to discipline.

MARCH 9 – *Forget all else in His presence*

When Amma thinks of love for God, the story of Vidura's wife comes to mind. Both Vidura and his wife were ardent devotees of Lord Krishna. Vidura once invited Lord Krishna to his house. He and his wife waited anxiously for the day of the Lord's visit. They thought of nothing but Krishna. They were thinking about how to receive him, what to offer him, what they were going to say to him, and so on. Finally, the day arrived. The time of Krishna's arrival drew close. Vidura's wife went to take a bath before the Lord arrived. It was while she was taking a bath that Krishna arrived, earlier than expected. A maid came and informed her of the Lord's arrival. Vidura's wife ran out, calling, 'Krishna! Krishna!' and approached the Lord. She had forgotten that she had just been having her bath. She brought fruits for the Lord and prepared a seat for him. And as she did these things she was continuously chanting, 'Krishna! Krishna!' In her state of devotion, she wasn't aware of anything else. She ended up sitting down on the seat meant for the Lord, while he sat on the floor! She wasn't aware of any of this. She peeled a banana. She threw away the fruit, and lovingly offered the peel to the Lord! He sat there smiling and relished the peel. It was then that Vidura came into the room. He was dismayed at the scene. His wife was sitting stark naked and dripping wet on Krishna's seat, while the Lord was made to sit on the floor! He couldn't believe his eyes. She was throwing away the banana and feeding Krishna with the peel! And Krishna was enjoying all this as if nothing strange was happening.

Vidura was furious. 'Oh, you wicked one, what do you think you're doing!' he shouted at his wife. It was only then that she returned to her senses and became aware of what she had done. She ran out of the room, and after a while she returned wearing newly washed clothes. She and Vidura made the Lord sit in his chair and they worshiped his holy feet as they had planned. They offered him the numerous delicacies they had prepared. She selected a beautiful banana, carefully peeled it, and offered it to him. When it was all over, Krishna said, 'Even though you performed all of those rituals exactly according to tradition, they couldn't equal the reception I received when I first arrived! What you gave me later didn't match the taste of the banana peel I first received!'

The reason was that Vidura's wife had completely forgotten herself in her devotion while she offered him the banana peel. My children, this is the kind of devotion we need, the kind that makes us forget everything in the presence of God.

MARCH 10 – *Bath in the river of Love*

When the obstructions of ego, fear and the feeling of otherness disappear, you cannot help but Love. You do not expect any return for your love. You don't care about receiving anything; you just flow. Whoever comes into the river of Love will be bathed in it, whether the person is healthy or diseased, a man or a woman, wealthy or poor. Anyone can take any number of dips in the river of Love. Whether someone bathes in it or not, the river of Love does not care. If somebody criticizes or abuses the river of Love, it takes no notice. It simply flows.

March 11 – *Helping others*

In harming others, we harm ourselves. Similarly, when we help others, we are helping ourselves.

March 12 – *A world made up of many petals*

This world is like a flower. Each nation is a petal. If one petal is infested, does it not affect all the petals? Does not the disease destroy the life and beauty of the flower? Is it not the duty of each one of us to preserve the beauty and fragrance of this one world flower from being destroyed? This world of ours is a big, wonderful flower with many petals. Only when this is understood and deeply ingrained in us, will there be any real peace and unity. The tug of war between nations is like the tug of war between the petals of a flower. Competition between the petals will only result in all the petals withering away. The entire flower will be destroyed. Division will only dissipate our energy and vitality; real power is to be found in unity, not in division.

MARCH 13 - *Death as a beginning*

People wonder why we die despite the presence of the supreme soul.

Death is only a parting, the end of the vehicle. The vehicle (the body) is weak. When we write a sentence, we end it with a full stop before starting another. Death is like that full stop. It is not an ending. It is a shift to something else. If you grasp this principle, death becomes a joyful, wonderful sensation just like diving into water. We simply move on to the next stage.

MARCH 14 - *Noble goodness*

Today's world needs people who express goodness in their words and deeds. If such role models can set an example for their fellow beings, the darkness now prevailing in society will be dispelled and the light of peace and non-violence will once again illumine the earth. Let us work together towards this goal.

MARCH 15 - *Tuning the chords of our life*

These days, our faith is like an artificial limb. It has no vitality. We have no heartfelt connection with faith, for it has not been ingrained properly into our lives.

This is a scientific age. Intellect and reason have reached great heights. But surprisingly, the most intellectually developed people still have great faith and reliance only in cars, TVs, houses and computers – all of which could stop functioning and perish at any moment. We are deeply attached to these things and to the small comforts they offer. If they are damaged or destroyed, we hastily engage ourselves in repairing them. Yet we do not realize that it is actually we who are most urgently in need of repair. For we have lost faith in ourselves. We have lost faith in the heart and its tender feelings. A man who shows great patience in repairing his computer and TV shows no patience in retuning the notes that are off-key in his own life.

Darkness is slowly enveloping the world. It is a pitiful scene we see all around. Having dissipated all their energy and vitality by running after objects of pleasure, people are collapsing. Man has gone beyond the reasonable limits set by nature. This does not mean that one should not enjoy the pleasures of the world. That is all right. But understand this great truth that the enjoyment and happiness you get from sensual pleasures and worldly objects are only a minute reflection of the infinite bliss which comes from within your own Self. Know that your true nature is bliss.

MARCH 16 – *Take refuge in the truth*

Amma has millions of children. If you depend only on Her external love, you will feel jealous whenever She is affectionate towards anyone else. The external

Amma you see now is like the reflection of a flower in a vessel filled with water. You can never make that flower your own, because it is only an image. To realize the Truth, you have to seek That which is true. Taking refuge in a reflection isn't enough, you have to take refuge in the real thing. If you love Amma, you should do so with the awareness of the Real Principle. When you fully understand the Real Principle, the mind won't attach itself to anything external. Only in this way will you be able to enjoy the state of bliss, forever.

MARCH 17 – Quench our thirst for love

How did love, which is the intrinsic nature and obligation of a human being, become a mask? It is when one denigrates oneself by acting without humility or compromise that love becomes a pretence. For example, if you just stand by a clear river and look, will your thirst be quenched? In order to quench one's thirst, one has to bend down to drink the water. Instead of doing this, if one remains standing upright and curses the river, what is the point? It is just as easy to fill ourselves with the crystalline waters of love if we surrender.

MARCH 18 – Give up selfishness

A man sits with a candle in front of his house at night. A sudden wind blows out the candle. It is only then that his eyes are opened to the beauty of the smiling full moon and the cool moonlight. No wind can extinguish the moonlight. Similarly, when we give up our selfishness, the bliss we receive in return is great and everlasting.

MARCH 19 – *Always forgive*

My children, you may wonder, 'Aren't we becoming like doormats? Don't we lose our sense of discrimination if we always forgive and so on?' On the contrary. It allows both sides to go forward. Only in those who understand this principle can a true attitude of selfless service be formed. True selfless service is done with a spirit of surrender. It is akin to a circle: it has no beginning or end, because it is love for the sake of love alone. With this attitude there are no expectations. In this state, we see all those who are working alongside us as gifts from God. This can happen only when love is present, and only then can we forgive others and forget their mistakes.

MARCH 20 – *Overcoming the mind's tricks*

Until now you have placed your faith in the mind. But the mind is like a monkey that jumps from branch to branch, from one thought to another, and will continue to do this until its last moment. Making the mind your companion is like befriending a fool –

it will always create some trouble; you will never find any peace. If we keep the company of fools, we will also become fools. It is foolish to put your trust in the mind and to follow the mind. Don't get trapped by the mind. We should always remember the goal – Self-realization. We shouldn't allow ourselves to be led astray by any distractions along the way.

MARCH 21 – *Our talents are a treasure*

Our God-given abilities are a treasure that is meant for ourselves as well as for the entire world. This wealth should never be misused and made into a burden for us and for the world. The greatest tragedy in the world is not death; the greatest tragedy is to let our great potential, talents and capabilities be underutilized, to allow them to rust while we live.

MARCH 22 – *Show your love*

Children should have the feeling that they are loved. Our love towards children should not be like honey hidden deep inside a stone.

MARCH 23 – *They know not grief*

A man was taking part in a fund-raising campaign. Knocking at the door of a wealthy household, he expected to receive at least a thousand rupees, but this family only gave him five! Furious, he refused to take the donation. A year later, he was still angry!

He pent up his anger inside. Because he didn't get what he expected, he couldn't even accept what was offered him. If he'd had no expectations, he wouldn't have been angry or suffered. He would have been satisfied with the little he received.

In this journey of life, if we adopt the attitude of a beggar, we can avoid this kind of suffering. A beggar knows he is a beggar, so he is not upset if he receives nothing when he knocks at a door; he is not sad because he knows that perhaps someone will give him something at the next house. Whether he receives some food, or whether he leaves empty-handed, he accepts this, because he knows it is part of life's journey. Therefore, he bears no grudge against anyone. When you are a true beggar, you consider everything as God's will. Be only bound to God, this is what Amma means. Truly spiritual people do not know grief.

March 24 – *Inner peace*
If we want to bring peace to the external world, first our inner world needs to be at peace. Peace is not an intellectual resolve. It is an experience.

March 25 – *We are all part of the Universal Consciousness*
We need to give up the notion that we are individuals, and act with the awareness that we are

part of the Universal Consciousness. Only then can we put compassion and non-violence fully into practice. You wonder if it is possible to do this. But even if we don't fully reach that state, shouldn't we at least strive as much as we can to love and to serve others, and keep that as our goal?

MARCH 26 - *Compassion is the expression of love*

Love is the inner feeling and compassion is its expression. It doesn't see the faults of others. It doesn't see the weaknesses of people. It makes no distinction between good and bad people. Compassion cannot draw a line between two countries, two faiths or two religions. Compassion has no ego; thus there is no fear, lust or passion. Compassion simply forgets and forgives. Compassion is like a passage. Everything passes through it, nothing can stay there. Compassion is love expressed in all its fullness.

MARCH 27 - *Act*

To stand passively by and watch as evil unfolds, without taking any action or feeling any concern, is an even greater evil.

MARCH 28 - *Effort is essential*

No one can reach the goal without effort. Effort is required in both worldly and spiritual life. However, it is divine grace that brings completion to the effort and gives it beauty, and a selfless attitude is what qualifies one for that grace.

My children, when you perform selfless service for the world, you may think, 'Because of all this work, I don't get even a moment to think of God. All my time is lost in work. Is my life going to be useless?' But those who perform selfless actions don't have to tire themselves looking for God anywhere, because God's true shrine is the heart of the person who does selfless service.

MARCH 29 – *Women and enlightenment*

Women have to wake up and arise! At present, most women are asleep. The awakening of the dormant power of women is one of the most urgent needs of our age. Not only should women in developing countries wake up – this applies to women all over the world. Women in countries where materialism is predominant should awaken to spirituality. And women in countries where they are forced to remain within the narrow walls of religious tradition should awaken to modern thinking.

MARCH 30 – *Liberating in work*

The work we do with the attitude that it is God's work will not cause any bondage.

MARCH 31 – *Life force exists in everything*

The life force that pulsates in the trees, plants and animals is the same life force that pulsates within us.

The same life energy that gives us the power to speak and to sing is the power behind the song of the bird and the roar of the lion. The same consciousness that flows in and through every human being lends its power to the movement of the wind, the flow of the river and the light of the sun.

APRIL

APRIL 1 – *Life is like a bridge*

If life is a bridge, birth and death are its two ends. We have no control over these two fundamental pillars of life. We are completely ignorant about them. As such, how can we logically claim the middle part, which we call 'life', as ours?

Similarly, childhood, adolescence, youth and old age do not seek our permission before they come and go. They just happen. Recognize this truth and perform actions that will uplift both you as an individual and society as a whole.

APRIL 2 – *God awaits us*

God is compassion. He waits at the door of the heart of each and every one of us.

April 3 - *Spiritual peace*

The aim of all spiritual practice is to be at peace, whatever the circumstances. All other experiences will pass, whether light, sound or form. If you have visions, these are temporary. The only permanent experience is absolute peace. This peace is the experience of a serene mind; this is the true fruit of spiritual peace.

April 4 - *Making the world more beautiful*

We should live our life in a manner that is helpful to ourselves as well as to others. God has given lightning just a few moments of existence. So too, a rainbow. Some flowers blossom just for a single day. The full moon lasts only till sunrise. A butterfly lives for only a few days. However, during their short existence, they give so much beauty and happiness to the world. Amma prays that we learn from their example and try to use our lives to make this world an even more beautiful place. Let us colour our lips with words of truth. Let us line our eyes with the kohl of compassion. Let us adorn our hands with the henna of good deeds.

April 5 - *Keep moments of solitude*

If you try to pump water to a higher level, you won't succeed if there is a leak at the bottom of the system. In the same way, we have to stop the leakage of the mental power that we have gathered, by giving up all our external interests. We need to spend time in solitude and purify our minds by getting rid of the bad habits we have accumulated in the past. To do so, we should avoid interacting with too many people.

April 6 – *Free yourself from fear*

Fear makes life equal to death; it weakens the power of our actions. It renders our mind a slave to selfishness and wickedness. The source of this fear is the feeling that 'I am weak'. This arises due to lack of understanding regarding the infinite power within us.

April 7 – *The vast field of the Self*

Complaints and sorrows arise only when you think you are the body. In the realm of the Self there is no place for sorrow. When Mother contemplated the nature of the Self, it became clear to Her that She was not a stagnant pond, but a free-flowing river.

Many people come to the river – the sick as well as the healthy. Some drink from the water; others bathe in it, wash their clothes in it, or even spit in it. It makes no difference to the river how people treat it – it keeps flowing. Whether the water is used for worship or for bathing, it never complains. It flows along, caressing and purifying those who enter it.

APRIL 8 – *Keep a steady mind*

Courageous are those who refrain from getting angry in situations where anger would be expected. When a person doing spiritual practice in solitude says, 'I don't get angry,' it doesn't mean anything, nor is it a sign of courage. Your negative tendencies won't necessarily die just because you are doing spiritual practice somewhere alone. A frozen cobra won't raise its hood and bite; but as soon as it is warmed by the sun, its nature changes. The jackal sits in the forest and makes a vow, 'From now on, I won't howl when I see a dog!' But as he comes out of the forest and catches the first glimpse of a dog's tail, his vow evaporates. We should be able to maintain our mental control even in the most adverse circumstances. That is where the success of your spiritual practice can be measured.

APRIL 9 – *Worship God in everyone and everything*

God is not confined to any particular place, but is all pervasive. God resides in all beings, animate and inanimate. God should also be worshiped in the sick and poor. God's nature is pure compassion. Lending a helping hand to a neglected soul, feeding the hungry, giving a compassionate smile to the sad and dejected – this is the real language of religion. We should invoke God's compassion in our own hearts and hands. Only then will we experience deep joy and fulfilment in life. Living only for oneself is not life, but death.

April 10 – *Get up!*

It is never a good practice to continue to sleep after sunrise. Do not stay in bed once you are awake, for it increases laziness and dullness.

April 11 – *When life becomes prayer*

God doesn't need anything from us. What does the Lord of the Universe lack? Why would the sun need a candle? The true offering to God is to go through life with awareness of the spiritual principles. Eating and sleeping only according to our needs, speaking only when necessary, speaking in a manner that doesn't hurt anyone, not wasting time unnecessarily, caring for the aged and speaking to them lovingly, helping children to get an education, in the absence of a regular job learning a trade and spending some of the income to help the poor – all these are different bones, of prayer. When we bring proper awareness into our every thought, word and deed, life itself is transformed into worship.

April 12 – *Every dawn waking*

Each dawn we are greeted with a new sunrise. At night when we forget everything and sleep, anything could happen to us, even death. Do we ever thank the Great Power that blesses us to wake up the next morning and function just as before without anything having happened to our body and mind? If we look at it in this way, shouldn't we be grateful to everyone and everything? Only compassionate people are able to express gratitude.

April 13 - *Tuning in to Divine consciousness*

A television station broadcasts various programmes, but we have to tune the TV properly to receive those programmes. If we don't select the right channel, why blame others for our not being able to see anything? God's grace is always with us. But to receive that grace, we first have to tune ourselves to the realm of God. If we don't bother to do this, there is no point in blaming God. As long as we are not in tune with God's realm, there will only be discordant notes of ignorance within us.

April 14 - *Why waste time worrying?*

If you are a student, learn your lessons with great attention, without brooding over whether or not you will pass the exam. And if you are constructing a building, build carefully according to the plan, without worrying about whether the building will stand or collapse.

Good actions bring good results. If a farmer sells

rice of good quality, people will buy it, and he will be properly rewarded for his work. But if he sells an adulterated product hoping for extra profit, he will be punished either today or tomorrow, and he will lose his peace of mind. So do each action with alertness and an attitude of surrender to God. Each action will receive its result in full measure, whether you worry about it or not. So why waste time worrying about the fruits of your actions? Why not use the time to think about God?

APRIL 15 – 'Make me love You!'

So, my children, your prayer to God should be 'Make me love You, and let me forget everything else!' This is the lasting wealth of life, the wellspring of bliss. If we develop such devotion, we have succeeded in life.

APRIL 16 – Mastery and enlightenment

When you press down a button, the umbrella unfolds. Similarly, by bowing your head down before a spiritual master, your mind can be transformed into the universal Mind. Such obedience and humbleness are not signs of weakness. Like a purifying water filter, the master purifies your mind and removes your ego.

Today, people's minds are weak, like a plant growing in a pot. If the plant isn't watered daily, the plant withers the very next day. The mind cannot be brought under your control without discipline. As long as you haven't mastered your mind, you need to abide by certain rules and restraints according to the master's instructions. Once you have mastered your mind, there is nothing to fear; for then the power of discrimination will awaken within you and lead you forward.

APRIL 17 – *Caring for Nature*

The destruction of Nature is the same thing as the destruction of humanity. Trees, animals, birds, plants, forests, mountains, lakes and rivers – everything that exists in Nature – are in desperate need of our kindness, of the compassionate care and protection of man. If we protect them, they, in turn, will protect us.

APRIL 18 – *No expectations, no suffering*

Regardless of whom we are helping, we should never expect any kindness in return. Sometimes, we may receive abuse in return. Having any expectation that someone will be kind to us in return will only cause us sorrow. Our mind should be like an incense stick that burns out while giving its fragrance to everyone, even to the one who burns it. This is what brings us to the feet of the Supreme Being. We should be of benefit even to those who harm us. Our minds should have the attitude of offering flowers in return for the thorns that are thrown at us. By developing our minds in this way, we can live in peace and harmony.

APRIL 19 – *Do not get lost in greed*

A dog is chewing a bone. When blood oozes, the dog thinks it is coming from the bone. Finally the dog collapses due to all the bleeding. Only then does it realize that the blood isn't coming from the bone, but from its own injured gums. This is what the experience of seeking happiness from external things is like.

APRIL 20 – *Yearn for God*

Shedding tears while praying is not a weakness. When we pray out of our longing for God, positive qualities are nurtured within us. Heartfelt prayer in which we cry for God steadies and focuses the mind, and the mind becomes one-pointed. Instead of losing energy, we gain energy through such concentration. Even though God is within us, our minds are not focused on God. Crying in prayer is a way of focusing the mind on God.

APRIL 21 – *The pure and the impure*

God is like the wind. The wind blows equally over flowers and excreta. For God, there are no differences such as purity or impurity. But we still have to be aware of those differences, for only then can we progress.

April 22 – *Reaching plenitude*

We gain everything by knowing who we are. A feeling of complete fullness, with absolutely nothing else to gain in life. That realization makes life perfect. Regardless of what we have accumulated, or are striving to acquire, for most people, life still feels incomplete – like the letter 'C'. This gap, or lack, will always be there. Only spiritual knowledge and realization of the Self (Atman) can fill the gap and unite the two ends, which will make it like the letter 'O'. The knowledge of 'That' alone will help us feel well grounded in the real centre of life.

April 23 – *A bird's-eye view*

When you are in a forest, you see all the different kinds of trees, plants and creepers in all their diversity. But when you step out of the forest and start walking away from it, looking back, all the different trees and plants gradually disappear, until at last you behold everything as one forest. Likewise, as you transcend the mind, its limitations in the form of petty desires and all the differences created by the feelings of 'I' and 'you' will disappear.

Then you will begin to experience everything as the one and only Self.

APRIL 24 – *This world exists thanks to love*

The world depends on love for its existence. If we lose our harmony and our capacity to love, the harmony of Nature will also be lost; the atmosphere will be poisoned and will no longer be conducive for seeds to sprout and for trees and animals to grow. The crops will fail, diseases will multiply, rainfall will decrease and there will be droughts. Therefore, children, love each other! Be righteous, loving, and virtuous for the sake of Nature. This will lead to the harmony of Nature. See the good in everyone. Do not harbour anger or jealousy towards anyone, and never speak ill of others. Think of everyone as being a child of the same Universal Mother, and love them as your sister and brother. Surrender all your actions to God and let His will prevail in everything.

APRIL 25 – *If at first you don't succeed, try again with consciousness*

If you fall, think only that you have fallen in order to get up. Don't just lie there thinking that it's quite comfortable! And don't feel shattered by the fall. You have to make an attempt to get up and go forward. When we write on a piece of paper with a pencil, we can use an eraser if we make a mistake, and rewrite our words. But if we make a mistake again and again in the same place and try to erase it, the paper may get torn.

April 26 – *Keep some truths secret*

There is nothing higher than the truth; it should never be forsaken. But all truths are not to be told openly to everyone. You have to look at the circumstances and determine whether it is necessary to reveal something. There may be occasions when something has to be kept secret even if it represents the truth. Take the example of a woman who has committed an error in a weak moment. If the world comes to know about it, her future will be ruined; her life may be in danger. But if her mistake is kept secret, she may avoid repeating it and be able to lead a positive life. In this case, it is best to keep the truth a secret, rather than reveal it. In this way it is possible to save the person's life and protect her family. But one should carefully weigh the situation before such a decision is made. However, this should never encourage anyone to repeat a mistake. The important thing is that what we say will benefit everyone. If something we might say could cause someone pain, we shouldn't say it even if it is the truth.

APRIL 27 - *Everything is precious*

Amma remembers certain things from her childhood. If she happened to step on a piece of paper that had been swept into the garbage, she would touch it and bow down to it. If she didn't do this, she'd receive a spanking from her mother. Amma's mother used to tell her that that paper wasn't just a mere piece of paper; it was Goddess Saraswati, the Goddess of Learning, Herself. In a similar way, Amma was taught that if she accidentally stepped on cow dung, she should touch it as a sign of her reverence. Cow dung helps the grass to grow. Cows eat grass and give us milk. We use that milk. Amma's mother taught her that we shouldn't touch a door sill with our foot. If we happen to step on it, we should touch it with our hand and bow to it. The reason for this is probably that, symbolically, the doorway is the entrance leading to the next stage in life. When you look at things in this way, everything becomes precious. Nothing can then be ignored or disrespected. So, we should look upon everything with respect and reverence.

APRIL 28 - *Men and women - the same consciousness*

Women and men should honour the heart with the same importance they give the intellect. They should strive to work in a way that reconciles intellect and heart, and be role models for each other. Then equality and harmony will come about naturally. Equality is not something external. A hen can never crow like a rooster. But can a rooster lay eggs? Even if there are external differences, it is possible to become of one mind. Electricity manifests in a refrigerator as coolness, in a heater as warmth and in a bulb as light. A television will not have the qualities of a light bulb, nor a light bulb that of a television. Nor will a refrigerator be able to do what the heater does and vice versa. However, the electric current that flows through all these appliances is one and the same. Likewise, although there may be differences between men and women, the indwelling consciousness is one.

April 29 - Worship God in all forms

We should pour water at the root of a tree, and not at the top, for only then will the water reach every part of the tree. In the same way, if we really love God, we will love all living beings in the universe because God dwells in the hearts of all beings. God is the foundation of everything. Therefore we should see God in all forms and love and worship Him in all forms.

April 30 - Act with self-abnegation

Every act that is done without regard for one's own comfort or interest is self-abnegation. Amma calls any action self-abnegation if it is done as an offering to God for the benefit of the world, without any sense of 'I' or 'mine', and with no regard for your own comfort. The struggle a person undergoes for his own benefit cannot be considered self-abnegation.

When your child is sick, you take it to the hospital. You'll walk to the hospital, if necessary, even if it's a very long way. You are ready to fall at the feet of any number of people to get your child admitted to the hospital. You'll take time off work. But since all these sacrifices are made for your own child, this cannot be considered self-abnegation.

People are prepared to go up and down the courthouse steps countless times just to fight for a tiny piece of land. But they are doing it for themselves. People work late and give up their sleep to get overtime pay. This is not self-abnegation. But if you sacrifice all of your comforts and come to the aid of another person, you can call it self-abnegation. Say that your neighbour's child is sick, and there is no one to be with him in the hospital; if you stay with that child, expecting nothing in return from anyone, not even a smile, that qualifies as self-abnegation.

Through such acts of sacrifice, you knock on the door that leads to the realm of the Self. It is through such actions that you gain entry into that world.

MAY

MAY 1 - *Pleasure and renouncement*

We should eat only to satisfy our hunger. Health experts suggest that to maintain good health, no more than half the stomach should be filled with food, one quarter with water, and the remaining quarter left empty. Spiritual science also explains how to maintain our mental health. The idea is not that we shouldn't partake of any sensual enjoyments, but that we should never become slaves of our senses or of the habits of the mind. We should be the masters of our mind and senses. Along with enjoyment, it is important to also practise some degree of renunciation.

Viewing the situation from all angles, we can clearly see that putting spiritual principles to work in our daily life is the only way to bring about fundamental changes in today's world.

MAY 2 – *Love the king*

If you pray to God only to have your wishes fulfilled, you won't find freedom from suffering. If you want your suffering to end, you have to pray for your desires to end, and for your faith and love for God to grow. Our love should not focus on the ordinary objects that the king's palace contains. We should love the king himself. Having chosen the king, all the treasures in the palace will be ours. When we pray to God, it shouldn't be for a job or a house or a baby. We should pray, 'God, I want You to be my very own.'

MAY 3 – *The perfection of giving*

All spiritual practices are done to develop in us the attitude of wanting to dedicate ourselves to the world. But Amma is ready to venerate those who don't have the inclination to practise any spiritual discipline, but are nevertheless willing to dedicate their lives to the world. The benefit gained through prayer can also be gained through selfless service. In selflessness one is complete. In that state, the limited individual disappears.

MAY 4 – *Looking from within*

These days, instead of looking outwards from the inside, we are trying to look inwards from the outside. In this way, we will not be able to see anything clearly.

May 5 – *Flee the fire of anger*

Another thing we should pay special attention to in life is controlling our anger. Anger is like a knife that is sharp at both ends. It cuts the one it is aimed at as well as the one who is holding it. How turbulent our minds become when we are angry with someone! The mind becomes so disturbed that we cannot sit, stand, or lie down in peace. Our blood heats up. This paves the way for all the diseases we didn't have until now. In the heat of our anger, we don't recognize the changes that take place within us.

May 6 – *Concentration*

To count each grain in a handful of sand, or to cross a river balancing on a tightrope, you need a great deal of concentration and attention. You should have that same amount of concentration and attention in everything you do.

May 7– *Supreme Union*

Once supreme love for God has awakened in the seeker's heart, the various restrictions and observances are no longer essential. Before divine love, all restrictions and barriers dissolve. For a true believer who possesses that love, there is only God.

Throughout the whole universe, such a seeker sees only God. Just as the moth flies into the fire and merges with the flames, the believer, in his or her love for God, becomes God in essence. The seeker, the universe itself – all is God. What rules and restrictions could apply to such a soul?

MAY 8 – *Live like a witness*

If you wish to enjoy the beauty of a swiftly flowing river – not only the water, but also the fish and other creatures and things that dwell in the water, everything comprising the nature of a river – it is best to sit beside the river and observe it. If you jump into the water, you may get carried away by the current and even drown, and you won't be able to experience the beauty of the river. Similarly, live like a witness, without getting caught in the flow of the mind. Learn to detach from it.

MAY 9 – *Revolutionary innovation*

In India too, women are waking up and springing to action. Until recently, women were not allowed to worship in the inner sanctum of a temple; nor could women consecrate a temple or perform Vedic rituals. Women didn't even have the freedom to chant Vedic mantras. But Amma is encouraging and appointing women to do these things. And it is Amma who performs the consecration ceremony in all the temples built by our ashram. There were many who protested against women doing these things, because for generations all those ceremonies and rituals had been done only by men. To those who questioned what we were doing, Amma explained that we were worshiping a God that is beyond all differences, Who does not discriminate between male and female. As it turns out, the majority of people have supported this revolutionary move. Those prohibitions against women were never a part of ancient Hindu tradition. They were in all likelihood invented later by men who belonged to higher classes of society, in order to exploit and oppress women.

MAY 10 – *Change oneself to change the world*

But change has to begin with the individual. When an individual changes for the better, the whole family benefits, and then society prospers. So, first, we ourselves should make an attempt to do good. When we change ourselves for the better, it influences everyone around us; it will bring about positive changes in them as well. We have to set an example. We should be kind and loving towards everyone. Only through selfless love can we bring about a transformation in others. We may not see any immediate changes, but we should never lose hope or give up our efforts.

MAY 11 – *Finding mutual concessions*

Today, people's love is rarely based on mutual understanding. Their hearts do not know each other. The wife doesn't understand her husband's heart, nor does the husband understand his wife's heart. No one is ready to compromise. This is how life proceeds. How can there be peace in such a life? Through spirituality we develop the readiness to understand and accommodate each other. The reason for all the failures in life is the lack of mutual give and take.

MAY 12 – *A mirror doesn't get attached*

Don't be afraid! Don't give any importance to bad thoughts when they arise. Suppose we travel on a pilgrimage by bus. We watch the scenery through the window – some of it is beautiful, some not. But regardless of how intriguing the sights before us are, we forget them as soon as the bus has passed them by. We don't stop the bus every time we spot something beautiful. We appreciate the beauty, but we continue forward without stopping, keeping our minds on the goal. Otherwise, we will never arrive. We need to focus on our destination. Let the thoughts that arise in your mind pass by like the scenery through the bus window. Don't allow yourself to be captured by them. Then, they won't affect you that much.

There are two sides to the mind. One side looks

intently towards the goal and yearns for realization. The other side looks only at the outer world. There is a battle raging between the two. As long as you don't identify with or give any importance to the thoughts that arise in the mind, there is no problem.

At present your mind resembles a mirror on the roadside, reflecting whatever passes by along the road. In the same way, the mind goes out towards whatever we see or hear. Yet, we lack one quality that the mirror has: even though the mirror reflects everything clearly, nothing affects it; everything vanishes as soon as it passes out of view. The mirror is not attached to anything. This is what our minds should be like. We should let go of whatever we see, hear or think about, then and there, like a passing sight along the road. We shouldn't be attached to anything. We should know that the thoughts that rise and fall belong to the mind, but do not affect the Self.

MAY 13 - *Serve selflessly*

We become eligible for God's grace only when we are able to love and serve all living beings without any selfish desires. We forget this truth. We forget our obligation to serve those who are struggling. We visit the temple and perform worship, but when we come out of that place and are confronted by those who are sick or unable to find work, and they extend their hands towards us for a little food, we ignore them or shout at them and drive them away. My children, true worship of God is the loving kindness we show the suffering.

MAY 14 – *A new vision*

The law of gravity existed before it was discovered. A stone thrown upward has always had to come down again. In the same way, consciousness is always present in us – now in the present moment – but we may not be aware of it. But to experience it, we need a new vision, a new eye, and even a new body.

MAY 15 – *Feeling*

Whatever the sound, learn to feel it as deep as you can. Feeling the sound, not merely hearing the sound, is what really matters. Feel your prayers, feel your mantra and you will feel God.

MAY 16 – *The true, the beautiful and the good*

When God's power shines through us, it manifests as truth, auspiciousness and beauty. When God manifests through the intellect, truth shines forth. When God manifests through action, He does so as goodness and auspiciousness. And when God manifests through the heart, beauty is the result. When truth, auspiciousness and beauty blend in our life, true strength awakens.

MAY 17 – *A strong mind*

The advantage of self-discipline must be understood in the light of the situations we face. When we face difficult situations, we have to proceed without our minds weakening and without faltering. Experiencing peace while sitting in meditation and feeling agitated when coming out of it doesn't befit a seeker. Anyone can sing without accompaniment. But the singer's skill with voice modulation in harmony with the keynote becomes evident only when singing to the accompaniment of a harmonium and keeping time. Similarly, true abidance for a seeker means keeping the rhythm and harmony of the mind, whatever the circumstance may be.

MAY 18 – *Grasp the present moment*

This is a benevolent gift that the ancient sages, through their grace, have given us. My children, begin to live in accordance with this knowledge, without wasting even a moment. Otherwise, this life will be meaningless. Don't think you can do this tomorrow, because tomorrow is truly only a dream. Even now we live in a dream – that's all it is. Only by waking up from this dream can we know what reality is. And it is to God that we awaken. We should feel assured of this, for only then can we awaken from this dream. Each passing moment is extremely valuable, and shouldn't be wasted. It is foolishness to postpone our awakening until tomorrow and sink back into the dream. Tomorrow is a question without an answer. It is like adding four and four and saying it totals nine; it will never be nine. Nothing is more valuable than this moment that we have now. Don't ever let it go to waste. Grasp the present moment and learn to laugh with an open heart.

MAY 19 - *Only take what you need*

Nature gives all her wealth to human beings. Just as Nature is dedicated to helping us, we too should be dedicated to helping Nature. Only then can the harmony between Nature and human beings be preserved. To pluck ten leaves, when only five leaves are sufficient, is a sin. Suppose two potatoes are enough to cook a dish. If you take a third potato, you are acting indiscriminately – you are committing an unrighteous act.

Using Nature for our needs cannot be considered wrong. But exploitation changes the whole set of circumstances. This makes our action an unrighteous one. First of all, we are unnecessarily destroying the life of the extra plant, animal or whatever it is that we exploit. Secondly, we deny it for someone else's use. Someone else could have used it, perhaps our neighbour who does not have anything to eat. Thus, when we exploit Nature, we are exploiting others. It is certainly a necessity to have a house to protect us from the rain and the sun. But we should not build a house in order to make a show of our wealth and luxurious lifestyle. An act becomes unrighteous or sinful when we perform it indiscriminately, without any alertness.

May 20 – *Show your love*

Love isn't something to be kept hidden inside; love should be shown at the proper times. The wife doesn't get happiness from the love that lies hidden in her husband's heart. Since you don't know each other's hearts, it's not enough to keep your love hidden inside your hearts. You have to show your love – with words and deeds. Amma is saying this for the sake of peace and harmony in family life. If you don't show your love, it is just like placing a block of ice in the hands of a person tormented by thirst. The ice cannot quench anyone's thirst. So, my children, you should go to each other's levels and love each other with open hearts.

May 21 – *Be patient and forgiving*

We should understand that life isn't just for winners, but also for those who lose, and we should be willing to give those who have failed a chance. We should forgive their mistakes. To be patient and forgiving is like lubricating an engine. It will help us to move forward. To dismiss those who have failed only once amounts to doing them the greatest harm.

The losers shouldn't be ridiculed; they should be encouraged. To maintain enthusiasm, encouragement is essential.

MAY 22 – *Light the lamp of faith*

We must never lose our inner strength. Only weak minds always see the dark side of everything and become confused. Those with optimism see the rays of God's grace in any kind of darkness. The lamp of this faith is within us. Light this lamp, it will shower light to guide each and every step we take.

MAY 23 – *Be aware of your power*

As long as you think you are the body, you are like a small battery whose power is easily drained. But when you know yourself to be the Self, you are like a giant battery connected to the cosmic power supply, which provides you with continuous and inexhaustible strength. When connected to God, the Self, the source of all power, your energy never diminishes.

You are able to tap into your infinite potential. Be aware of your own immense power and strength.

You are not a meek little lamb, you are a majestic, powerful lion.

MAY 24 – *Never hurt anyone*

Those who always indulge in fault-finding will never progress spiritually. Do not harm anyone by thought, word or deed. Be compassionate towards all beings.

MAY 25 – *Break the hidden chains*

Like a bird with clipped wings in a golden cage, we are imprisoned in our own minds. We are bound by the chains of name and fame, position and wealth, and those chains are covered with beautiful flowers. The question here is not one of freedom, but how to break the chains that bind us. In order to do this, we have to see the chains attached to us, and not the flowers. The flowers and decorations are only superficial. If we look more closely, we can see the chains that are hidden by the flowers. We need to see the prison as a prison, not our home. Only then will our minds leap eagerly towards freedom.

MAY 26 – *Choose the music of the soul*

Whether you spend your time laughing or crying, time will go by anyway. So you might as well laugh! Find a reason to laugh every day. Laughter is the music of the soul.

MAY 27 – *Putting what you have learned into practice*

It is a state in which you see everyone as your own Self. That state should become our very nature. We become the flower, rather than contemplate the flower. We should all try to blossom. This is what we should make of our lives, and what our studies should be directed towards. Memorizing something is not that difficult; putting what you have learned into practice is difficult. The rishis [sages] of long ago demonstrated great spiritual truths through the examples of their lives. These days, people engage in verbal disputes after having read and memorized the words of the sages.

MAY 28 – *The multiple forms of God*

Real devotion is being able to perceive the deity, not only in the temple, but also in every living being, and to serve everyone accordingly. If your beloved deity is Krishna, you should be able to behold Krishna in every temple, whether it is a Shiva temple or a Devi temple. Children, do not think that Shiva will get angry if you don't worship Him in a Shiva temple, or that the Divine Mother will withhold Her blessings if you don't praise Her in a Devi temple. One and the same person is called 'husband' by his wife, 'father' by his child, and 'brother' by his sister. A person doesn't change when others call him by different names. In the same way, all the divine names are the names of the One Supreme Being. He knows your mind. He knows that you are calling Him, no matter what name you may use.

MAY 29 - *All paths lead to silence*

Some people may ask if prayers can't be done in silence. For some people it may be necessary to read in silence, while for others reading aloud is more effective. We cannot tell someone who reads aloud when studying, 'Don't read so loudly! You should read quietly, like me!' Some people get more concentration by praying aloud, while others prefer to pray quietly. Similarly, for different types of people different spiritual paths are required. All paths lead to the ultimate stillness.

MAY 30 - *Avoid making the same mistakes*

There is no sin that cannot be washed away with repentance. But this shouldn't be like the bath of an elephant! The elephant bathes and emerges out of the water, only to pour dust all over itself again without delay. This is how many people behave with their mistakes.

May 31 – *A beginner's humility*

Become humble. Remain a beginner till the end, like a child endowed with tremendous faith and patience. That is the best path. Such should be our attitude towards life and the experiences life brings to us. Then, we will keep on learning. Our bodies have grown in all directions, but not the mind. For the mind to grow and become as big as the universe, we should become a child.

JUNE

June 1 - *Be determined*

If this moment is lost, it is a great loss indeed. If you want to meditate, do it this instant. If there is a task that needs to be done now, it should be started at this very moment and not be postponed until a moment later. This is the state of mind we must adopt and the determination we must possess.

June 2 – Teaching certain values

Tomorrow's world will be shaped by today's children. In their tender minds, it is easy to cultivate universal human values. If you walk through a field of soft, green grass a few times, you will quickly make a path; whereas it takes countless trips to forge a trail on a rocky hillside. The teaching of universal spiritual values should be a standard part of the general education, not only the responsibility of the family. This should not be delayed further, for if there is a delay, the future generations will be lost to the world.

JUNE 3 - *Rub away our sharp edges*

Those who spend all their time living in solitude, doing only spiritual practice are like a tree in the scorching heat of a remote desert. The world doesn't benefit from its shade. Such people ought to go out and, living in the midst of the world, try to develop the attitude of seeing God in everyone and everything. If you put rocks of different shapes in a container and tumble them around, the rocks will rub against each other and lose their sharp edges. They will become nice and smooth. Only those who succeed in the midst of a world full of diversity can claim to have succeeded.

JUNE 4 - *Patience is the door to happiness*

We also need patience in life because patience is the very foundation of life. If we force open a bud, we will never know the beauty or fragrance of the flower. Only if it opens naturally will we experience this. Similarly, if we wish to enjoy the beauty of life, we cannot do without patience. For those who want their lives to be filled with happiness, patience is the most important quality they need.

JUNE 5 – *No pride, no shame*

God cannot be attained without giving up the sense of pride and shame. Feelings of pride and shame are creations of the mind. Only by breaking those chains that tightly bind the mind can we reach the feet of God.

JUNE 6 – *Start working now*

Amma remembers a story. In a certain country anyone could become king, but each king could rule for only five years. After that, he was taken to a deserted island and left there to die. There were no human beings on the island; there were only beasts of prey that would immediately kill and devour the king. Even though they knew this, many people came forward wanting to be king out of a desire to enjoy the power and pleasures of that position. As each one ascended the throne, they were elated. But from then on, there was only sorrow; for they feared the day they would be torn to pieces and eaten by the beasts on the island. Because of this, each king was filled with turmoil and never smiled. Though every luxury imaginable was available to them – delicious food, servants, dance, and music – they weren't interested in any of it. They weren't able to enjoy anything. From the moment they assumed power, they saw only death in front of them. They had come for happiness, but not a moment was free of sorrow.

The tenth king was taken to the island when his allotted time was over and, like all the previous kings, he was consumed by the wild beasts. The next person who came forward to be crowned as king was a young man. But he wasn't at all like the other kings. He wasn't the least unhappy after assuming power. He laughed with everyone, he danced, he went on hunting trips, and often rode around inquiring about the welfare of the people. Everyone noticed that he was always joyful.

Finally, his days in power were coming to an end, but there was no change in his demeanour. His subjects said to him, 'Your Majesty, the time for you to leave for the island is drawing near, but you don't seem sad at all. You are joyful even now!'

The king replied, 'Why should I be sorry? I'm ready to go to the island. There are no longer any dangerous animals there. When I first became king, I learned how to hunt. I then went to the island with my troops and we hunted and killed all the beasts of prey. I cleared the forest on the island and turned it into farmland. I dug wells and built some houses. Now I shall go and live there. Having given up this throne, I shall continue to live like a king, because everything I need is on the island.'

We should be like that king. We should discover the world of bliss while we are in this physical world. Instead, almost everyone can be compared to those earlier kings. They don't have a moment free from anxiety and anguish about tomorrow. There is sorrow today and sorrow tomorrow.

But if we spend each moment today with discernment, we won't have to suffer tomorrow – all our tomorrows will be days of bliss.

JUNE 7 – *Be love*

Once we develop the attitude that 'I am love, the embodiment of love', then we need not wander in search of peace; for peace will come in search of us. In that expansive state of mind, all conflicts dissolve, just as the mist fades when the sun rises.

JUNE 8 – *Evening offering*

During the twilight hours, impure vibrations permeate the atmosphere. This is the reason why we chant the divine names or sing sacred songs during that particular time. If we fail to pray at that time, our worldly tendencies will grow stronger. At that time the ego is most predominant. Only by taking refuge in God, can we destroy the ego. But these days, people watch TV or surf the Internet at that hour.

JUNE 9 – *We will not falter*

Spirituality is the principle that allows us to face each situation and crisis in life with a smile. Those who aren't familiar with this principle will be shattered by even a minor obstacle. If a huge firecracker goes off when we are standing somewhere unawares, it will startle us; but if we know that it's about to go off, we won't be shocked. If we are aware, we won't falter when we are confronted by adverse circumstances.

June 10 – *Conquer the ego*

If we persist in cultivating the ego, nothing will be gained. By being humble, we gain everything.

A selfless, desireless attitude helps us to remove the ego. That is why unmotivated actions are given so much importance.

June 11 – *Rid yourself of negative feelings*

It is not necessary to go up to everyone and show them your love; it's enough not to have any negative feelings – none whatsoever. Real love is the complete absence of any negative feelings towards anyone. By removing all such negative feelings, the love, which is ever present within you, will shine forth. Then there are no distinctions, no sense of difference. Haven't you seen how those who loved each other yesterday despise each other today? So their love was never real. Where there is attachment, there is also anger. Our aim is to have neither attachment nor anger. That is real love. Selfless service is the most noble form of love.

June 12 - *Constant practice*

My children, no matter how long we study the scriptures, regardless of how many times we say to ourselves that we have the strength to overcome any problem, if we haven't brought our minds fully under control we will still falter when faced with difficulties. We may hear countless times that we are not the body, mind or intellect, that we are the embodiments of bliss, but we forget this when we encounter even trivial problems. Constant practice is therefore essential if we want to be strong in the face of difficulties.

June 13 - *A prayer to waylay thoughts*

Chanting a mantra is a way to make the mind do our bidding, taking advantage of its own nature. If a hundred thoughts arise in the mind, we can reduce them to ten by chanting a mantra. You may wonder if there won't be thoughts in your mind while you chant this sacred formula. Even if there are, they are not that important. Thoughts are like a baby: when the baby sleeps, it is easy for the mother to do the household chores; but once the baby wakes up and starts crying, it is difficult for her to work. Likewise, the thoughts that arise while we chant are not much of a problem; they won't bother us.

June 14 – *True innocence*

'Innocence' is a greatly misinterpreted word. It is even used to refer to non-reactive and timid people. Ignorant and illiterate people also are usually thought of as innocent. Ignorance is not innocence. Ignorance is a lack of real love, discrimination and understanding, whereas true innocence is pure love endowed with discrimination and understanding. It is divine energy. Even in a timid person, there is ego. A truly innocent person is a truly egoless person; therefore he or she is the most powerful person.

June 15 – *Leave no room for anger*

We should forgive and forget the faults of others. Anger is the enemy of every spiritual aspirant. Anger causes loss of power through every pore of the body. Whenever the mind is tempted to get angry, we should control it, and with a firm resolve say to ourselves, 'No!' We should then go to a secluded spot and chant our mantra. Thus the mind will quiet down by itself.

June 16 – *Nothing is permanent*

Birds perch on tree twigs, where they eat and sleep. But they know that if the wind blows, the twig they are perching on could break. So they are constantly alert, ready to fly away at any moment. The things of this world are like such twigs; they may be lost at any moment. In order not to be overcome with grief when this happens, we have to hold fast to the Supreme Principle.

If the house is on fire, none of us will say, 'Let's put it out tomorrow!' We'll put out the fire immediately. Today our lives may be full of sorrow, but instead of brooding, ruining our health and wasting time, we should try to find a solution.

My children – that which is with us now won't be with us forever. Our house, wealth and property won't be with us always. In the end, none of these things will be our companions. Only the Supreme Being is our eternal companion. Amma isn't saying that we should give up everything or that we should feel aversion towards anyone. Amma means that we should recognize that nothing is permanent. We should live a life of detachment.

This is the only way to find peace in life.

JUNE 17 – *God is not a house servant*

Let God become part of every aspect of your life. Those who cannot build a separate room for worship can set aside at least a section of a room for prayer, meditation and spiritual study. This place should be used only for spiritual practices. God should not be relegated to a space beneath the stairway. We should live as God's servants, and never put Him in the place of a servant.

JUNE 18 – *An inexhaustible source of love*

If you give someone ten rupees out of the hundred you have, only ninety rupees will remain. But love is different. No matter how much love you give, it can never be exhausted. The more you give, the more you will have, like an endless spring that flows into the well as you draw water. People are born to be loved. They live for love. Yet, it is the one thing not available today. A famine of love plagues the world.

JUNE 19 – *Express our gratitude*

We always say, 'Give me this! Give me that!' But we haven't learned to say, 'Thank you!' We have to learn to express gratitude in all circumstances.

JUNE 20 – *The art of being*

Look at Nature. Look at that tree over there, how blissfully it sways in the wind. And look at those birds. They're singing, forgetting everything else. And that stream over there – how merrily it flows, singing melodiously. And those plants – and the stars, the sun, and the moon. Everywhere there is only joy. Being in the midst of all of that joy, why are we the only ones who grieve? Why are only we unhappy? Contemplate this and you will understand. None of those elements of nature has an ego. Only we do. 'I am this and that, I want to become that, I want that' – this is what we think about all the time. But this 'I' we are so preoccupied with will not accompany us when we die. If we hold fast to that 'I', there will be nothing but suffering.

So, my children, give up that 'I' and arise! Then you will be happy and rejoice. Be happy, my children. Only this moment is ours.

JUNE 21 – *Faith is the foundation of everything*

If we stay firmly committed to what we really believe, we can experience God. Faith is the foundation.

JUNE 22 – *The authentic disciple*

When we talk about a true master, we don't mean just an individual; we mean the Divine Consciousness – the Truth. The master permeates the entire universe. We need to understand this, for only then can we advance spiritually. A disciple should never be attached to the physical body of the master. We should broaden our view so that we see every sentient and insentient being as the master, and serve others with devotion. It is through our bond with the master that we acquire this expansiveness. The mind of a disciple who matures by listening to the master's words and watching the master's deeds rises to that plane without the disciple being aware of it. On the other hand, the service rendered by a person who desires physical proximity to the master for purely selfish reasons is not real service to the master.

The disciple's bond with the master should be such that it becomes impossible to be away from the master even for a moment. At the same time, you should be expansive enough to serve others, and should do this to the point of forgetting yourself. Such is the true disciple who has absorbed the real essence of the master.

June 23 – *The great lesson in letting go*

Whether you call it surrender, the present moment, here and now, moment-to-moment living or another term, they are all one and the same. The terms may differ, but what happens inside is the same. Any form of spiritual practice we do is to help us learn the great lesson of letting go. True meditation is not an action; it is an intense longing of the heart to be one with the Self, or God.

June 24 – *Taking care of others*

However high your position in life may be, always have the attitude that you are just a servant of your fellow beings. Think that God has placed you in a fortunate position as an opportunity to help those in need. Humility and modesty will then spontaneously dawn within your heart. When you work with the attitude that you are serving God, your work will become a form of spiritual practice. Be friendly and loving towards everyone at your workplace – superiors and subordinates alike. The way you treat others determines how the world will treat you.

JUNE 25 – *Acquire true knowledge*

My children, real knowledge is to know the mind, to know the Self. It teaches us how to apply the divine principles in our lives. Hardly anyone tries to acquire that wisdom now. Yet, this is what we need to learn above all else. Learn how to hunt before you go hunting, and you won't waste your arrows; nor will you be in danger of becoming prey to wild animals. If you understand how we are meant to live, your life can be truly meaningful.

JUNE 26 – *Let hearts expand*

The intellects of people have grown so much that nowadays they cannot live without machines that do everything for them. Because of this, no one gets enough exercise. To maintain your health, you have to find time to exercise. When you consider this, you will see that the comforts gained in one way actually make us weaker in other ways. Today people are constantly feeling tense. In spite of all the comforts and commodities we have, each moment of our life is filled with tension. Selfishness has grown to this extent. As the intellect grows, the heart withers. The day is long gone when we felt that the sorrows of others were our own sorrows. Today people don't hesitate to place others in difficult circumstances for the sake of their own happiness. If this is to change, the heart has to expand along with the intellect.

JUNE 27 – *Take refuge in God*

It is possible to go through life without believing in a Supreme Being. But to be able to go forward with firm, unfaltering steps when faced with a crisis, we need to take refuge in God. We should be ready to follow God's path. A life without God is like a court case in which two lawyers are arguing without a judge being present. The hearing will go nowhere. If they proceed without the judge, no ruling is possible.

JUNE 28 – *Respect all beliefs*

It is not wrong for each person to believe that their faith is right. However we should give others the freedom to their beliefs as well. When we force our religion on others, religions born of love become causes for bloodshed. We should not allow religions that are intended as songs of peace to create disharmony and violence.

JUNE 29 – *An open heart*

God is love and compassion towards the suffering. If one has such a heart, there is no need to pray to God.

JUNE 30 – *The fire of words*

It is sometimes said that fire is the deity of speech. The nature of fire is heat, light and smoke. Just as fire gives heat and light, each word of ours should give energy and knowledge to others. But it shouldn't taint their minds the way smoke blackens a room.

JULY

July 1 – *God is bliss*

My children, you should pray for God alone. Only then will you ever be completely fulfilled. Whatever falls into sugar becomes sweet. Similarly, because God is bliss, our closeness to God gives us bliss. If you catch the queen bee, all the other bees will follow her. If you take refuge in God, all spiritual and material gains will be yours.

July 2 – *Speaking ill of others is speaking ill of oneself*

Laughing at the mistakes committed by others isn't real laughter. We should be able to burst out laughing at our own mistakes. We should be able to laugh deeply, forgetting everything – remembering only the Supreme Truth. That is true laughter, the laughter of bliss. But are we able to do this?

Today, we laugh mostly when we recall the defects of others or are saying negative things about others. My children, speaking badly of others is to malign ourselves.

July 3 - *Qualities to develop*

There are three elements which make a human being human:

- The intense desire to grasp the sense and depth of life by using the intellectual faculty to discern,
- The miraculous capacity to give love,
- The ability to be joyous and give joy to others.

Religion should help us to develop these three qualities fully. This is how religion and human beings will reach perfection.

July 4 - *A sweetly fragrant garden*

If you are looking after a wild animal, you have to watch it all the time to make sure it doesn't run away. If you let it loose, you have to follow it everywhere, otherwise it could escape. When you feed it, you have to stay with it until it has finished eating. You are never free of toil. But the keeper of a garden has only to stay at the gate and watch to ensure that nobody steals the flowers. He can also enjoy the fragrance. Likewise, if you go after worldly life, your mind will bother you constantly; it will never remain steady. Spirituality, on the other hand, allows you to enjoy the beauty and fragrance of life without turmoil or botheration.

JULY 5 – *The world's true riches*

Patience, awareness and attentiveness are the real wealth in life. A person who has gained these qualities can succeed anywhere – that is how important they are. When you develop these qualities, your internal mirror, which helps you to see the impurities within yourself and remove them, becomes clear of its own accord. You become your own mirror; you will know how to remove your impurities without needing anyone's help. You attain the ability to purify yourself. When you reach that stage, you don't see anyone as inferior to yourself. You never argue unnecessarily. You don't resort to empty words. Your greatness is reflected in your actions.

JULY 6 – *Unconditional love*

Normally relationships lack real love. In relationships of ordinary love, there are two – or you could say there are three – the lover, the beloved and love.

In real love, however, the lover and beloved

disappear, and what remains is an unbroken experience of pure, unconditional love.

JULY 7 – *How can we still be proud?*

A person calls from the top of the stairs, 'I will be right down!' But he hasn't taken more than five steps when he collapses of a heart attack.

Not even the next moment is in our hands. Once we truly understand this, how can we be egotistic? As we breathe out, there is no guarantee that we will ever breathe in again. It is God's power that carries us through every moment. As we come to realize this, we will naturally feel humble.

JULY 8 – *When individuality dissolves*

Because a river is filled with water, we see two riverbanks, and we talk of this side and that side. But if the river runs dry, we see that there's only a continuous stretch of sand; the two banks and the river bed form part of the same ground. In the same way, the concept of 'you' and 'I' arises only because we continue to have a sense of individuality. Once the individuality disappears, everything is one and the same – whole and perfect.

JULY 9 – *What we seek is already within us*

'All seeking should stop' means seeking happiness in the outside world should stop, because what you are seeking is within you. Stop running after the objects of the world and turn inward. There you will find what you are seeking.

You are both the seeker and the sought. You are searching for something that you already have.

JULY 10 – *Do not think you are chained*

Self-realization cannot be bought. A change must take place in your attitude, that's all. People are misled and think their binds are real.

A cow was tied up in her shed every night. One day, instead of tying her up, the owner just put the cow inside the stable and closed the door. The rope was lying on the floor. The next day, when the owner opened the door to let the cow out, the cow did not move. He tried to push her, but she refused to budge. He used a stick, but to no avail. 'Usually I tie the cow up, but last night I didn't. What if I pretend to untie her?' he thought. He took the end of the rope and pretended to untie it. The cow left the stable at once.

Humans are like this. They are not tied up, but think they are. We must dispel this illusion. Simply understand that you are absolutely not chained up. For bonds to be untied, they must first exist. But without the help of a true master, you will not be able to correct this erroneous notion. The master's task is to convince you that there are no bonds in the first place.

July 11 - *Love is stronger than fear*

True love is the state of complete fearlessness. Fear is part and parcel of the mind. Therefore, fear and genuine love cannot go together. As the depth of love increases, the intensity of fear slowly decreases.

Fear can only exist when you are identified with the body and mind. Transcending the weaknesses of the mind and living in love is Godliness. The more you love, the more divinity is expressed within you. The less love you have, the more you move away from the centre of life. Fearlessness indeed is one of the greatest qualities of a true lover.

July 12 - *Integrating spiritual principles*

Every religion has two aspects: one is its philosophical teachings as explained in the scriptural texts; the other is spirituality. The former is religion's outer shell, the latter its inner essence. Spirituality is awakening to one's true nature. Those who make the effort to know their True Self are the truly faithful. Whatever one's religion, if one understands the spiritual principles one can attain the ultimate goal, the realization of one's true nature. On the contrary if we fail to absorb the spiritual principles, religion will be nothing more than blind faith, shackling us.

July 13 – *Rules that liberate*

If you drive your car just any way you feel like, disregarding the rules of the road, you will probably have an accident and could even die. There are rules of the road which have to be followed. Similarly, not only has God created everything; He has laid down rules for everything, and we have to live according to those rules.

Eat only what is necessary. Speak only when necessary. Sleep only for as long as you need. Spend the remaining time doing good deeds. Do not waste a single moment in life. Try to make your life beneficial for others as well.

July 14 – *Awakening from the dream*

The dream is not separate from the dreamer. But we have to wake up to see that what we have experienced is a dream. Although everything is God, we perceive everything around us as being separate, because we haven't awakened yet to that awareness.

We feel attachment towards some things and aversion towards others. Because of this, happiness and sorrow have become the nature of life. When we awaken to our true essence, there is no 'I' or 'you' – everything is God, and only bliss remains.

JULY 15 – *Seek inner beauty*

A big party was being held. All the guests were dressed in expensive clothes and jewellery. Then one of the guests arrived wearing ordinary clothes. The doorman refused to let him in. The man went home and returned wearing a formal suit. This time he was allowed to enter. When he reached the dining table, he removed his jacket and placed it in front of a dish. He took off his hat and put it next to a glass, and placed his tie in front of a teacup. The other guests thought he was crazy. He turned to them and said, 'When I arrived here in my ordinary clothes, they wouldn't let me in. When I came in this suit, I was immediately allowed to enter. From this I gather that it wasn't I, but my clothes that were invited to this party.'

This is what the world is like today. People place their faith in external appearances. Rare are those who look for the inner beauty.

JULY 16 – *Immutable depth*

Each thought, each emotional outburst, and each desire is like a pebble thrown into the mental lake. The incessant thoughts are like ripples at the surface of the water. The undulating surface makes it impossible to see through the water clearly. You never allow the mind to be still. Either there is the craving to fulfil a desire or there is anger, jealousy, love and hatred. And if nothing is happening in the present, memories of the past come creeping in. Sweet pleasures, bitter memories, joyful moments, revenge, something will always arise. As soon as the past withdraws, the future comes with beautiful promises and dreams. Thus the mind is constantly engaged. It is always occupied, and never vacant.

What you see is only the surface. You perceive only the waves on the surface. Yet, because of the movement on the surface, you mistakenly think that the bottom is moving too. But the bottom is still. It cannot move. You are superimposing the movement of the surface – the ripples of the thoughts and emotions – on to the still bottom, the underlying bottom. The movement caused by thought waves belongs only to the surface; it belongs to the mind.

JULY 17 – *Realize the Self*

If we keep Self-realization as our final goal in life, we will shape all our thoughts and actions in a way that will help us to attain it, won't we? We will always be aware of our true destination. Someone travelling from one place to another may make several stops to have a cup of tea, or to eat, but he or she will always return to the vehicle. Likewise in life, we may stop many times and do various things. However, we mustn't forget to reboard the vehicle carrying us along the spiritual path and to remain seated with our seat belt tightly fastened.

July 18 – *Distinguishing the ephemeral from the eternal*

Live today with great care and alertness, and tomorrow will be your friend.

Devotion is important. But to pray and then to talk badly about others is not devotion. We should try to see everyone as God – that is devotion. Doing good deeds with great attention is also devotion. What Mother calls devotion is the ability to discriminate between the eternal and the ephemeral. This is what is needed.

July 19 – *Stay in your centre*

A householder takes care of only his wife and children; he only has to pay attention to their problems. But a spiritual person must carry the burden of the whole world. He mustn't falter in any situation. He must be firm in his faith and spiritual wisdom. He cannot be weak. His life should never be influenced by anyone else's words or deeds.

But today people are not like that. If someone utters a few insulting words out of anger, they are ready to kill that person, right there and then. If they can't take revenge immediately, they'll constantly be thinking of a way to get back at him. The balance of their lives rests on a few words from the lips of others. A real spiritual being isn't like that at all. He trains himself to stand firmly centred within himself. He learns what life is really about. Spiritual life is impossible without real discrimination and detachment.

July 20 – *Great souls*

If we all turn our backs on a person, thinking only of the wrongs he or she has committed, what future does that person have? On the other hand, if we perceive the little good that is still there and encourage that person to cultivate that quality, he or she will be uplifted. This could have such an effect that he or she may even become a great person. Sri Rama was willing to prostrate before Queen Kaikeyi, who was responsible for his banishment to the forest. Christ washed Judas's feet, even though he knew that Judas was about to betray him. When the woman who had once thrown dirt on Prophet Muhammad fell ill, he came to her and nursed her without being asked to do so. Such are the examples shown to us by the great souls. The easiest way to experience constant peace and happiness in life is to follow the path they have shown us.

July 21 - *Selfless service*

The truth is that not even for a moment can we not be doing something. If we are not active physically, we are active mentally. While asleep, we perform actions in our dreams. And our breathing and other bodily functions continue automatically. There is no way to avoid action. So then, why not do something that will benefit the world in some way? Selfless actions weaken our innate undesirable tendencies. Only if our thoughts, words and deeds are good can we overcome the tendencies we have accumulated so far.

In olden days, the spiritual masters gave tasks, such as gathering firewood, watering plants and washing clothes to the disciples who came to them to study the sacred texts. Selfless service is essential for transcending selfishness and attachment to the physical body. So, no one should be idle or discourage those who work.

July 22 - *Love and life are indivisible*

A scientist may claim he is trying to find the truth of the empirical world through an analytical approach. He dissects things in order to analyse how they function. If he is given a kitten, he is more interested in using the animal for research than loving it as a pet. He will measure its rate of breathing, its pulse and blood pressure. In the name of science and the search for truth, he will dissect the animal and examine its organs. Once the kitten has been cut open, it is dead. Life disappears and any possibility for love is gone. Only if there is life, is there love. In his search for the truth of life, the scientist unwittingly destroys life itself. Strange!

July 23 - *Make time for spiritual seeking*

What meaning is there to life if you cannot set aside at least one hour a day out of the twenty-four, to think about God? Think of how many hours you spend on the Internet, watching TV, gossiping and doing other useless things! Children, you can definitely set aside an hour for spiritual practice if you really want to. This should be your most valuable time.

July 24 - *Selfish people are never at peace*

By its increasing selfishness, humankind is digging its own grave. People are digging where they stand and will fall into that hole. They do not realize this. Those who want twice as much of everything – whether food or wealth – are in fact stealing what belongs to others. Because of their greed, others don't have enough to meet their needs. Selfish people don't experience any peace during their lives or after they die.

July 25 – *We receive what we give*

When a change takes place in us, it is reflected in others as well. My children, always remember that we receive only what we give. The heart pumps blood into all the cells of the body. The cells get nutrition in this way. The blood then flows back into the heart. If there is any obstacle to this, life itself becomes threatened. Like the heart, we need to learn not only to receive but also to give back. Only when we give, do we receive in return. In the chain of life, a deficiency in one link will affect the others. We need to understand that our every smile, word and deed has the power to spread sunshine to the lives of many others. So, we need to make sure that our actions create joy and contentment not only for us but also for others.

July 26 – *Our enemies are within*

Our enemies are not outside; they are within. We are our own enemy. The way we've become slaves to our desires, and our general misunderstanding about the nature of life are all weaknesses that make us limited.

July 27 – *A love free of all expectations*

In worldly relationships, we may experience suffering. If one person's love diminishes, the other person may get angry. The reason is that the relationship is based on hopes and wishes, on desires and expectations. But when we turn to God, it's completely different because we don't expect anything in return for our love. Yet, in that love without expectations we are given everything.

July 28 - *Become an inspiring example*

My children, even if someone who performs selfless actions doesn't find the time to repeat or chant the least prayer, he or she will attain immortality. Like nectar, such a person is beneficial to others. A selfless life is the greatest spiritual discourse anyone can give. Others can see and emulate it.

July 29 - *Love, trust and faith*

Modern people focus on reason and intellect, and often hold the view that love and faith are blind concepts. But Amma says that reason is blind – because when there is nothing but logic and reason, life itself withers away. So, our focus should be on love, mutual trust, and faith.

Imagine a society built on reason and intellect alone! In such a society there will be only machines that look good, move by themselves, and talk. Yet, are not love and faith the foundations of life?

Manure and fertilizer should be placed at the roots of the rose bush. Don't heap them on top of the fragrant blossoms and ruin the sweet scent!

Apply reason and intellect where they belong. Don't allow reason and intellect to ruin the love and faith that give beauty and fragrance to life!

July 30 – *Growing*

A seed has to go down into the soil for its potential form as a plant to emerge. Only through modesty and humility can we grow. Pride and conceit will only destroy us. Be loving and compassionate with the firm attitude that you are the servant of everyone.

July 31 – *The best way to worship God*

Amma remembers a story. A man decided to enter politics. But a friend told him:

'Don't go into politics, because if you do you'll have to give away everything you have.'

'Fine, I will do that.'

'If you have two cars, you will have to donate one of them.'

'That's definitely no problem!'

'If you have two houses, you'll have to give one of them away.'

'Sure, I'll do that too.'

'Also, if you have two cows, you'll have to give one of them to someone who doesn't have a cow.'

'Oh, no! That's impossible!'

'Why not? You have no problem giving away

your car or your house. Then why do you hesitate to give away just a cow?'

'Because I don't have two cars or two houses. But I do have two cows!'

This is the nature of people's generosity nowadays. They are more than willing to donate what they don't have, but unwilling to donate what they do have! My children, this is not what our generosity should be like. If we can help someone – even if we have to struggle a little to do so – this is the greatest way of worshiping God.

AUGUST

August 1 – *Overcome suffering*

Suppose someone verbally abuses you and you react by sitting in a corner crying. You are unhappy because you accepted the abuse. If you don't accept it, it becomes that person's problem, not yours. So you have to disown it. If you act with discrimination in this way, you will attain freedom from suffering.

When suffering comes our way, we should try to overcome it, rather than weaken at the thought of it. Certain sages of old learned the essential truths and applied them in their lives. If we heed their words and live according to the scriptural guidelines, we can move through any situation without faltering. Spiritual knowledge is far more essential in life than worldly knowledge, for it teaches us how to live in this world.

AUGUST 2 – *Oppose wrong action*

If our tolerance makes another person more egotistic, it is best to give it up. But we should be careful not to harbour any feelings of vengeance or resentment towards that person. We shouldn't be against the individual, only against the wrong actions he or she commits.

AUGUST 3 – *Get to know your inner world*

There was once a function to inaugurate a supercomputer. After the inauguration, the participants were told they could ask the computer any question and it would come up with the answer in seconds. People did their best to ask the computer the most complicated questions relating to science, history, geography and so on. As soon as each question was posed, the answer would pop up on the screen. Then a child stood up and asked the supercomputer a simple question: 'Hello supercomputer! How are you today?' But this time, there was no response; the screen remained blank! The computer could answer questions about everything except itself.

Most of us live in a state similar to that of the computer. Along with our understanding of the outer world, we need to develop the knowledge about the inner world.

August 4 – *Remember God always*

Many types of waves travel in the atmosphere around us. Thoughts are also waves. This is why we say that each thought and word should be expressed with care. It is said that the tortoise hatches its eggs with its thoughts, the fish with its gaze, and the hen through body contact. Our thought waves are also powerful. If we get angry at someone who has not done anything wrong, he or she will feel hurt and say, 'Oh God, I don't know anything about it! Why are they saying all this?' The wave of sorrow coming from that person will reach us and be captured by the subtle aura surrounding us, and the aura will absorb it. It will darken our aura like smoke covering a mirror. Just as smoke hinders light from falling on a mirror, the darkness caused by that wave of sorrow will prevent us from receiving divine grace. This is why we are asked to give up bad thoughts and to cultivate thoughts about God. By cultivating a constant remembrance of God, we become like God.

August 5 – *Changing our state of mind*

There is a way to overcome difficult situations, and that is to change our state of mind. This is the only way to truly find joy. It is impossible to change the external environment completely to suit our needs. So we need to change our state of mind to suit the environment. This is possible only through spiritual practices.

AUGUST 6 – *The eternal source*

What happens when you draw water from a well? The well is immediately replenished by the water of the spring beneath it. The spring will keep on filling the well. The more water you draw, the more water comes from the spring. So you could say that the water in the well keeps growing. The well is full and it remains full because it is forever connected to the spring. The well keeps on becoming perfect. It keeps expanding. The human body is a very limited instrument. It cannot contain the unlimited consciousness. However, like the well, once you are connected to the eternal source of Shakti, our consciousness will keep expanding within us.

AUGUST 7 – *Understanding and tolerance*

The problem arises when we say, 'Our religion is right; yours is wrong!' This is like saying, 'My mother is good; yours is a prostitute!' Love and compassion are the very essence of all religions. What then is the need for us to compete?

AUGUST 8 – *A master's presence*

Children, if we pass through an incense factory, the scent will remain on us afterwards. We don't have to work there, or buy any of the incense, or even touch anything – all we have to do is enter the place and the fragrance will linger on us, without any effort on our part. In the same way, when you are in the presence of a mahatma, a change takes place within you, without you even being aware of it. The time you spend with a mahatma is invaluable. Being in the company of dark-minded people, on the other hand, is like entering a coal mine. Even if we don't touch the coal, our bodies will be black when we come out.

One can easily find the opportunity to do tapas (austerities) for many years, but the chance to be with a mahatma is extremely rare and hard to come by. Such an opportunity should never be wasted. We should be extremely patient and try to get the most out of the experience. A mere touch or glance from a mahatma can benefit us far more than ten years of tapas.

August 9 – *Laughing at our own weaknesses*

Those who can see and laugh at their own weaknesses and shortcomings have discernment.

August 10 – *Moving through the layers of our emotions*

Spirituality is not a journey to somewhere else – it is coming back home, a return journey that brings us back to the original source of all our lives. During this process, we must go back through the layers of emotions we have so far accumulated. This is the cause of our suffering. If we remain open while moving through these layers, we will transcend them, and be led to peace and supreme bliss at last.

August 11 – *Get to work!*

Think of how hard people work to pass an exam or to get a job! Yet no one tries to know themselves, to attain the experience of everlasting bliss. Whatever time is left of our earthly existence should at least be spent for that purpose.

August 12 – *A world to be shared*

Humans must understand that they are not the only species with the right to live. So many species have already disappeared! It is not enough to be good and compassionate towards humans, it is necessary to manifest these virtues towards all living beings.

August 13 – *The sole principle*

We can mould clay into the shape of a donkey, a horse, a mouse or a lion. Even though they are different in name and form, they are, in fact, nothing but clay. So the mode of perceiving the universe through different forms and names has to be abandoned. It is, in fact, the one Supreme

Principle that has transformed itself into all those forms. Everything is God. There is nothing that is not God.

August 14 - *The spiritual master's duty*

You cannot know the Truth without totally destroying the veil of ego. The master will test the disciple in various ways to ascertain whether he or she has come to the master out of a short-lived surge of enthusiasm or out of love for the spiritual goal. Those tests can be compared to surprise tests in the classroom; there is no advance warning. It is the master's duty to measure how much patience, renunciation and compassion the disciple has, and to test whether he or she becomes weak when faced with certain situations, or has the strength to overcome them. The disciples are expected to provide the world with leadership in the future. Thousands of people may come to them one day, placing their complete trust in them. The disciples have to possess enough inner strength, maturity, and compassion to live up to that trust.

August 15 - *It's pointless to worry*

Those who have surrendered to God don't have to worry about anything. We should never approach anyone with a desire in mind, for that will only bring us suffering. Let us take refuge in God alone.

He will bring us everything we need. Everything comes automatically when needed.

AUGUST 16 – *Take risks*

- To laugh is to run the risk of looking stupid.
- To cry is to run the risk of appearing sentimental. To hold out your hand to someone Is to risk committing.
- To show your feelings is to risk being vulnerable. To express your ideas and dreams to the masses is to risk losing them.
- To love is to risk not being loved in return.
- To hope is to risk losing hope.
- To try is to risk failure.
- But it is necessary to take risks because the biggest risk of all would be to take none.
- He who risks nothing achieves nothing, has nothing and is nothing.
- You may avoid suffering this way.
- But it is impossible to learn, feel, change, grow, love or live.
- Shackled by fears, such a person is a slave who has given up their freedom.
- Only those who take risks are free.

AUGUST 17 – *Surrender to God*

There is only one way to know God: by offering oneself fully.

AUGUST 18 – *Trim down our needs*

Renunciation should be part of our lives. If you are accustomed to buying ten new outfits of clothes every year, buy one outfit less this year, and two less next year. Thus you will gradually reduce your wardrobe to no more than what you really need. The money saved in this way by ten people would be enough to build a home for someone really in need. Others will also change when they observe your selflessness and your virtuous way of life. Cut down on luxuries, not only on clothing but everything else as well, and use the money you save thereby for charitable purposes.

AUGUST 19 – *He beats in everyone's hearts*

The truth 'I exist' is self-evident. You may deny God by saying 'God is just a belief,' but existence cannot be refuted. That existence, that Cosmic Power, is God. God has no separate hands, legs, eyes or body other than ours. He moves through our hands, He walks with our legs, He sees through our eyes, and it is He who beats within the heart of each one of us.

AUGUST 20 – *Bow down humbly*

When we bow our heads before a spiritual master, we are not focusing on that individual, but on the principles that the master embodies. We are bowing down to that ideal, so that we may also reach that level. Only through humility can we ascend. There is a tree within every seed. But if a seed remains in the storeroom claiming to be a tree, it will just turn into fodder for a mouse! The real nature of the seed emerges after it bows down and goes beneath the soil.

August 21 – *Fan the flame of compassion*

When natural calamities occur, people's hearts open up, transcending thoughts of caste, religion and politics. Yet, the non-judgmental attitude and compassion people express during such situations come and go as quickly as a flash of lightning. If instead, we can manage to keep that flame of compassion ablaze within, it can dispel the darkness surrounding us.

August 22 – *Heal our wounds*

Love is the very foundation of life. Ninety per cent of the physical and mental problems we face stem from the pains and sorrows of the past. Each of us goes through life with many unhealed wounds. Medical science hasn't found a medicine that can cure those wounds. But there is a single cure for them all: that we open our hearts to each other.

When mutual love and respect develop, your problems will recede. Love is the very ground of life. The cause of all our problems today is that we consciously or unconsciously ignore this. If the body needs food in order to grow, love is what the soul needs.

So, my children, love one another and become one.

August 23 – *Giving way is moving forward*

Today, people's minds are full of vanity. Our effort should be directed towards destroying the ego within us. That means being perfectly tuned to others. Say that two cars are heading towards each other on a narrow road. If both drivers refuse to yield and give way, neither of them can move forward. But if just one of them is prepared to back up a little, they can both proceed.

Here, the one who compromises and yields and the one who receives that gesture are both able to go forward. This is why it is said that to yield is to go forward. It will uplift both the person who yields and the one who receives the courtesy. We should always look at the practical side. The ego is always a hindrance to progress.

August 24 – *Rooting our life in the Truth*

Let your life be firmly rooted in the Truth. Abstain from telling lies. In this dark age of materialism, adherence to the Truth is the greatest austerity. You may have to tell a lie now and then to protect somebody, or to sustain harmony, but be careful not to tell lies for your own selfish purposes.

AUGUST 25 – *Love without expecting anything in return*

Life should be lived as if we were performing a duty. Then we won't succumb to sadness if others turn against us or forsake us. If someone we have loved more than our own life suddenly turns against us, we won't go to pieces. There will be no reason for us to despair. If there is a cut on your finger, it won't heal if you just sit and cry. Nor will it help if you cry when you lose your wealth or your kith and kin. Crying will not bring them back. But if we can understand and accept the fact that those who are with us today could leave us tomorrow, we can live happily, free from sorrow. This doesn't mean that we shouldn't love anyone. On the contrary, we should love everyone. But our love should be selfless. We should love without any expectations.

AUGUST 26 – *Become like beggars*

In fact, we should think of ourselves as beggars. A beggar comes to a house seeking alms. The people in the house may say, 'There are no alms here. Go away!' But no matter what they say, he doesn't open his mouth. He thinks, 'I am only a beggar. There is no one on this earth with whom I can share my sorrows. Only God knows my heart.' If he were to try to explain this to that family, they wouldn't understand – he knows that. So if someone gets angry with him, he walks away in silence and goes to the next house. If they too are angry, he again continues on to the next house, without complaint.

This is what we should be like. As soon as we take on the attitude of a beggar, the ego largely disappears. We will feel that we have no refuge other than God, and then the negative tendencies will fall away by themselves. Only by trying to become smaller than the smallest, does one become greater than the greatest. By developing the attitude of being everyone's servant, one becomes the master of the world.

AUGUST 27 – *Reject no one*

Anyone can reject others, but to accept everyone is difficult. Only through love can we lead others from wrong to right. If we disown someone for his mistakes, he will only continue to commit them.

AUGUST 28 – *Our life in danger*

Amma does not ignore the fact that there may be an economical gain to be had from the use of chemical fertilizers. With those chemicals, we temporarily get better harvests. But in another way, they are killing us. Some may say that more abundant harvests will solve the problem of famine, but with this sort of reasoning they miss a very important point, which is that many cells die in the bodies of those who eat vegetables and cereals which have been grown using toxic substances.

We don't take the small prick of a needle seriously, but if we are continuously pricked, it could end in death. The consequences of toxic substances entering our bodies are similar to that. Each of our cells is in the process of dying. Only when we fall dead will we understand the seriousness of the matter.

August 29 – *Equal love for all*

Mother doesn't know how to be partial in Her love. If a lamp is lit in front of a house, everyone who comes there will receive an equal amount of light, neither more nor less than anyone else. But if you keep the doors closed and stay inside, you will continue to be in the dark. To remain in the dark and then to blame the light is of no use. If you want the light, you have to open the doors of the heart and come out.

August 30 – *Cultivate detachment*

It is difficult to develop detachment by overindulging. Amma isn't saying it is impossible, but the detachment gained through enjoyment is temporary. So we have to consciously cultivate an attitude of detachment towards worldly things. We may like payasam (a sweet rice dish), but if we consume a lot of it we'll feel satiated, and later we'll want twice as much. Thus, we can never turn away from sensory pleasures by attempting to satisfy them permanently. Only by consciously adopting an attitude of detachment can we move away from worldly things.

When you are travelling to a new place, there won't be anything to worry about if you have a reliable map. Similarly, if you use the principles of spirituality as a guide and live your life accordingly, you will never be overwhelmed by any crises. You will know how to foresee and deal with any situation. Spirituality is the practical science of life. It teaches us the nature of the world, how to understand life and live fully in the best way possible.

SEPTEMBER

September 1 – *Overcoming sadness*

My children, if you can't completely control your sadness, meditate and say a prayer for a short while or read some scriptural text. Tie the mind down to some task that you like instead of letting it wander. Your mind will then quiet down. In this way, you won't waste time or ruin your health.

September 2 – *Managing your time*

Yes, you have to love discipline as much as you love God. Those who love God also love discipline. We should love discipline more than anything.

Those who have the habit of drinking tea at a regular time will get a headache and feel other discomforts if they don't get their tea. The habit that they had yesterday will automatically make itself known at a certain time today. Similarly, if we make a schedule for all our activities and strictly observe it, it will develop into a habit; it will even remind us at the right time of whatever we have to do.

SEPTEMBER 3 - *A mother's responsibility*

Woman is the creator of the human race. She is the first Guru, the first guide and mentor of humanity. Think of the tremendous forces, either positive or negative, that one human being can unleash upon the world. Each one of us has a far-reaching effect on others, whether we are aware of it or not. The responsibility of a mother, when it comes to influencing and inspiring her children, cannot be underestimated. There is much truth in the saying that there is a strong woman behind every successful man. Wherever you see happy, peaceful individuals; wherever you see children endowed with noble qualities and good dispositions; wherever you see men who have immense strength when faced with failure and adverse situations; wherever you see men who possess a great measure of understanding, sympathy, love and compassion and who give themselves to others – you will usually find a great mother who has inspired them to become what they are.

SEPTEMBER 4 - *A true servant*

What everyone needs is peace. But a majority want to be king. No one wants to be a servant. How can there be peace then? Won't there be war and conflict? A true servant is the real king.

SEPTEMBER 5 – *Maturity*

Maturity, in truth, is the ability to continue learning our entire lives. It does not come with age, but with selflessness and an attitude of acceptance that is totally devoid of prejudiced conceptions.

SEPTEMBER 6 – *'May noble thoughts and ideals come to us from everywhere'*

All the great religions have infinite beauty and wisdom to share. We should create opportunities for people everywhere, especially young people, to learn not only about their religion, but those of others, and to become appreciative of their noble ideals. Instead of trying to increase the number of followers, religions should create an environment in which one may wisely accept the noble ideals of any religion. Let us go beyond religious conversion and work to eliminate narrow-mindedness and division. There is a prayer in the scriptures of India that says: 'May noble thoughts and ideals come to us from everywhere.' Let it be the slogan of religions for the new millennium.

SEPTEMBER 7 – *Seek good in everything*

The honeybee looks for nectar wherever it goes. Nothing else can attract it. But a common fly prefers to stick to excrement even in a rose garden. Even now our minds are like common flies. That has to change. We have to develop a mind that seeks only the good in everything, just like the honeybee that seeks only the nectar wherever it goes.

SEPTEMBER 8 – *Like the fragrance of incense*

We should be ready to offer everything, like an incense stick that burns itself out while spreading fragrance everywhere.

SEPTEMBER 9 – *The poorest of the poor*

There are three groups of people in today's world. The first group consists of the poorest people who have nothing. Amma knows many such people who come here. They don't even have one decent piece of clothing, so they come here wearing borrowed clothes. Countless people struggle because they can't afford to thatch their roofs or get treatment when they are ill, or pay for an education. They themselves don't know how they manage to survive each day. Then there is the second group of people. They have a little bit of money, which more or less covers their needs. They feel compassion for those who are struggling, but they cannot do anything about it. The third group is different from the first two. They have a hundred times more wealth than they need. They are intelligent; they run businesses and earn a fortune, but they spend their money only to enhance their own comforts and happiness. They don't care about those who are suffering. About them it can be said that they are truly the poorest of the poor.

SEPTEMBER 10 – *Pure consciousness*

True sannyasins cannot be categorized. They are beyond. If you say such-and-such a person is very simple and humble, still, there is 'someone' who is feeling simple and humble. In the state of sannyas, that 'someone' which is the ego, disappears. Normally, humility is the opposite of arrogance. Love is the opposite of hate. Whereas a real sannyasin is neither humble nor arrogant – he or she is neither love nor hate. One who has attained sannyas is beyond everything. He or she has nothing to gain or to lose any more.

Someone once asked a mahatma:

'Who are you?'

'I am not,' he replied.

'Are you God?'

'No, I am not.'

'Are you a saint or a sage?'

'No, I am not.'

'Are you an atheist?'

'No, I am not.'

'Then who are you?'

'I am what I am. I am pure awareness.'

September 11 – *Surrender to Him*

If we walk on a thorn and it pierces the sole of our foot, all the tears we may shed would not remove the thorn or lessen the pain. My darling children, this is why you should surrender everything to God and be strong! Be full of courage!

September 12 – *Be ready to act*

It usually takes less time to demonstrate something through action than to really get it across with words. We should be willing to take action, without waiting to see whether or not anyone will be there to help us. Then, people are bound to join in and help. If we just stand aside blaming and criticizing others, we are just polluting our minds. So, my children, we need to take action, and not just talk. Change is possible only through action.

September 13 – *Our tears are marks of union with God*

A child will pester his mother to make her buy what he wants. He'll keep following her around and he won't stop crying until he has the desired object in his hand. We have to pester the Divine Mother like that. We have to sit there and cry. Don't give Her a moment of peace! We should cry out, 'Show Yourself to me! Show Yourself!'

Anyone will cry when that longing comes to them. If you can't cry, make yourself cry, even if it takes some effort. Such tears are not tears of sorrow. They are a form of inner bliss. Those tears will flow when the individual soul merges with the Supreme Spirit. Our tears mark a moment of oneness with God. Those who are watching us may interpret it as sorrow. For us, however, it is bliss.

SEPTEMBER 14 – *Neither birth nor death*

The day the concept that we are born disappears, we have reached God's door. The realm of the Supreme Being lies beyond both life and death.

SEPTEMBER 15 – *Eliminate the darkness of our time*

All the members of a same family will probably not be of the same nature or mental calibre. There may be one person who acts and speaks without discrimination, or who gets extremely angry, thereby upsetting the entire household. But in the same family, there may be one person whose nature is quiet and calm. He might be a person who is endowed with humility, sharp discrimination and a great clarity of vision. Now the question is who or what maintains the integrity and harmony of the family? Without much deliberation, one can easily reply that it is the latter's qualities of humility, discrimination and goodness that hold the family and its members together.

One's person's anger and lack of discrimination are balanced by another person's calmness, humility and prudence. Had the characteristics of the angry, indiscriminate family member prevailed, the family would have disintegrated long ago. Likewise, even though today's world is confronting a great threat, it is the patience, love, compassion, self-sacrifice and humility of the sages which sustain and preserve the harmony and integrity of the world. The darkness of our age can be completely eliminated, if in each family there is at least one member who is dedicated and willing to adhere to the essential principles of true religion.

SEPTEMBER 16 – *God's loving presence*

No matter how far away a man's beloved may be, looking at a handkerchief gifted to him by her gives him so much joy. The man is not enjoying the cloth or embroidery of the handkerchief; he is enjoying the memory of his beloved. Similarly, no matter what form we imagine God to have, what we are actually experiencing is God's loving presence.

SEPTEMBER 17 – *Nature is at the end of her tether*

Scientific inventions are highly beneficial. But they should not be against Nature. The constant harm done by human beings has destroyed Nature's patience. She has begun to retaliate. Natural calamities are greatly increasing. Nature has commenced Her dance of final dissolution. She has lost Her balance owing to the unrighteous actions perpetrated against Her by humans. This is the main cause of all the suffering that human beings are undergoing during this present age.

September 18 – *One step at a time*

You may wonder, 'What is the point of one person struggling alone in society, in a world so full of darkness?' Each of us has a candle, the candle of the mind. Light that candle with the flame of faith. Don't worry about how you will manage to cover such a great distance with such a small light. Just take one step at a time. You will discover that there is enough light to illumine each step along the way.

September 19 – *The material world is perishable*

The scriptures tell us that Shiva burned Kama, the God of desire, in the fire emanating from his third eye. Today, we consider material things as real, as eternal; believing they belong to us, we focus our attention on them exclusively. When the third eye of knowledge opens, we understand that everything is perishable, and that only the Self is eternal.

SEPTEMBER 20 – *Know how to forget*

Success in life depends on the ability to forget what is not required in the present moment.

SEPTEMBER 21 – *Conserve your vital force*

To observe two hours of silence each day is very beneficial. If you are also able to observe silence one day a week, it will greatly help your spiritual progress. When you are in silence, the loss of energy will be minimal, even though thoughts may continue in the mind. It is through talking that we lose much of our vital force.

SEPTEMBER 22 – *Life is an adventure*

As a child goes through every stage of growth – when he tries to turn over, when he learns to crawl, when he begins to walk, etc. – he is like a soldier who will never accept defeat. Nowadays, however, by the time he grows up, crosses middle age and becomes a senior citizen, he becomes business-minded. Everything, including his relationships, become like business deals. Who is responsible for this? It is our society, our parents, our elders, our educational system, and our blind imitations. All these create fear, anxiety and cowardice. Humanity loses the strength to see life as an adventure or challenge that has to be faced with courage. The mind becomes neither capable of acknowledging the existence of others nor of considering their feelings. There are seven billion people on the face of this planet. However, almost no one thinks of anyone else. There is no friendship, no real family, no unity. We have strayed from the herd, each one of us rampaging like a rogue elephant.

SEPTEMBER 23 – *A crystalline river*

When we make God a part of our lives, our lives, and also the lives of others, will be sanctified. We then begin to experience peace and contentment. Think of a river that is full and pure. We are the ones that benefit from it. With the water from that river we can clean our dirty gutters and canals. A stagnant, putrid pond can be purified by connecting it to the river. God is like a crystalline river. By cultivating a relationship with God, our heart becomes so expansive that it encompasses the whole world. In this way we come closer to the Self and we benefit others as well.

SEPTEMBER 24 – *An icy heart*

Once, four men were travelling by boat to attend a religious conference when they were caught in a storm and had to take shelter on a deserted island. It was a bitterly cold night. The temperature had fallen below freezing. Each traveller carried a matchbox and a little bunch of firewood in his pack, but each one thought that he was the only one with firewood and matches.

The first man thought, 'Judging from the medallion round that man's neck, I would say he is from some other religion. If I start a fire, he will also benefit from its warmth. Why should I use my wood to warm him?'

The second man thought, 'That person is of the country that has always fought against us. I wouldn't dream of using my wood to make him comfortable!'

The third man looked at one of the others and thought, 'I know this guy. He belongs to a sect that always creates problems in my religion. I am not going to use up my wood for his sake!

The last man thought, 'This guy has a different colour of skin to mine, and I hate that! There's no way I am going to use my wood for him!'

In the end, not one of them was willing to use his wood to warm others, and so, by morning, they all froze to death. In reality, their cause of death was not the external cold. They died because of their icy hearts. We are becoming like these men. We quarrel in the name of religion, caste, nation and skin colour, without showing any compassion towards our fellow beings.

SEPTEMBER 25 – *The handicap of anger*

The deeper cause of wars and the increasing acts of terrorism we are seeing in the world today is the hatred in the minds of individuals. Storing up hatred for your enemy is like swallowing poison and waiting for your enemy to die. Hatred destroys our peace of mind.

When we see a person who is physically handicapped in a wheelchair, it is easy to feel compassion. People who are unable to control their anger suffer from a similar handicap, even though it is not visible. In the same way we feel compassion for a physically handicapped person, we should also feel compassion for a person who has the handicap of anger.

SEPTEMBER 26 – *Equanimity*

Understand the nature of life and act with wisdom, without collapsing when obstacles arise, and without being submerged by joy when circumstances are favourable.

SEPTEMBER 27 – *Radiate strength and beauty*

A rainbow appears and disappears in the sky within minutes. However within that short span of time, the rainbow is able to make everyone happy. Just like the rainbow which appears so briefly in the infinite sky, our lifespan, which appears for just a brief moment within the endless span of time, is also very short and insignificant. As long as we live in the world, our greatest and foremost duty is to be of some benefit to others. Only when goodness awakes within the individual will his or her personality and actions attain beauty and strength.

SEPTEMBER 28 – *Always keep the Goal in mind*

It is not difficult for you to think about your parents, relatives, friends or your favourite food. You can see them in your mind's eye the moment you remember them, and you can hold them there for as long as you wish. This is possible because of your long association with them. You don't have to teach or train the mind to think about worldly things, because the mind is used to them. You have to build a similar attachment to God. That is the purpose of prayer, meditation and teaching. Constant effort is needed, however; and with that effort, the form of your Beloved Deity, and the prayer pertaining to that form, will appear in your mind just as naturally as worldly thoughts do.

Children, don't be disheartened if you are not getting any real concentration in the beginning. If you try constantly, you will definitely succeed. You should always have the attitude, 'Only God is eternal. If I don't get to know Him, this life will be fruitless. I must see Him as soon as possible!' There are no obstacles on the path of a person who is constantly aware of the goal. For him, all situations are regarded as favourable.

SEPTEMBER 29 – *Extreme vigilance*

With every deed, word and glance of ours, and even with every thought, we have to be very careful. Every one of our thoughts, words and deeds has its own consequences. Every good or bad action of ours affects many others.

SEPTEMBER 30 – *The harmonious unity of the world*

The universe is one, not many. Man has divided the world into fragments, not God. It is man, who, through his thoughts and actions, creates turmoil and disintegration in the natural and harmonious unity of the world. Each atom is a building block of this universe and is intrinsically connected to every other atom. The planet where we live is not an isolated identity functioning separately from the universe. Everything is part of the Whole. When something good and elevating happens somewhere, those vibrations are reflected in the one Universal Mind. In the case of an evil act, negative vibrations will be reflected.

OCTOBER

❦

OCTOBER 1 – *'Come into my arms'*

In a village there was a beautiful statue of a great master with his arms outstretched. On a plaque beneath the statue, these words were inscribed: 'Come into my arms!' One day, a terrible riot took place in the village, there was a lot of destruction everywhere, and the statue was damaged – the arms were broken off. The villagers loved the statue and were very much upset about the damage. They gathered together and decided to make new arms for the statue. But an old man stood up among them and said: 'No, don't worry about making new arms for the statue. Let him be without arms.'

The villagers wondered, 'But what about the plaque underneath? It says: "Come into my arms!"' The old man replied, 'That is no problem. Just below the words "Come into my arms", you should add, "But I have no other arms than yours!"'

'Come into my arms, but I have no other arms than yours,' – that is what God is constantly telling us.

OCTOBER 2 – *The spirit of religions*

Many religious practices cater to the needs of the times in which they came into being. While dealing with the problems of this modern age, we should be prepared to re-examine those practices and make changes in accordance with the times we are living in now. No religious leader or saint has ever said that love and tolerance are to be offered only to the believers in one's own religion. They are universal values. What the world needs today is not religious propaganda, but the focus on helping people to imbibe the essence of religion.

OCTOBER 3 – *Why not be attached to God?*

If we can so easily become attached to anything in the world, why can't we become attached to God? Our tongues know how to talk about everything; why can't we teach our tongues to chant our prayer? If we can do this, not only we ourselves, but also those around us, will find peace.

OCTOBER 4 – *Solid foundations*

Because of parents' inability to properly mould their children, the power of destructive forces in society grows stronger with each generation. If we wish to change this, we should also acquire an understanding of the spiritual principles. As we enter family life, our knowledge of those principles will help us take each step along the right path.

If we build a house in a muddy area without first laying a firm foundation, even a gentle wind could cause the house to collapse. Similarly, if we base our family life only on materialism, the relationships within the family could crumble when the family is faced with even small problems. But if we build our family life on the solid foundation of spirituality, we can weather any storm. There should be no lapse on the part of parents in explaining spiritual principles to their children and acting as role models.

OCTOBER 5 – *Let us bow down*

We should eliminate the egotistic notion that our life will become fruitful through human effort alone. We should bow down. Only then will grace flow into us.

OCTOBER 6 – *Consciousness and attention*

Never think that you are working for your boss or for a company. Do your duty with the attitude that you are serving God. Then your work will not be just a question of putting in time to earn a salary; you will be sincere and attentive in your work.

The first qualities that a spiritual aspirant should cultivate are total dedication and full attention to the work at hand.

OCTOBER 7 - *The hand of the spiritual master*

Everything has its own codes, rules and inherent nature – and we should live in accordance with them. The masters have laid down the rules and methods for each type of spiritual practice. An appropriate method of spiritual practice should be adopted after taking into account the seeker's physical and mental disposition. The same method isn't suitable for everyone.

Anyone can learn theories by reading a book. But to be successful in practical tests, you need the assistance of a learned instructor, because it is difficult to master the practical aspects of a subject on your own. In the same way, the seeker needs a competent master who can guide him or her on the spiritual path.

OCTOBER 8 - *Grace*

The more dedicated you are, the more open you remain. The more open you are, the more love you experience. The more love you have, the more grace you experience.

Grace is openness. It is the spiritual strength and the intuitive vision that you can experience while performing an action. By remaining open to a particular situation, you are letting go of your ego and narrow-minded news. This transforms your mind into a better channel through which divine energy can flow. That flow of energy and its expression through our actions is grace.

OCTOBER 9 – *Preserving our spiritual strength*

Children, your mind is tied up with many different things. Spiritual life requires a great deal of discipline and self-control. It is like taking an ounce of oil and pouring it into a hundred containers, one after the other. In the end there is no oil left – only a thin film sticking to the insides of all the containers.

Children, you do your spiritual practices, but then you get involved in a variety of things. All the power you have gained through concentration is lost by your diversions. If you could only see unity in diversity, you would not waste so much energy. If you manage to see everything as God's essence, you will not squander your spiritual strength.

OCTOBER 10 – *Finding joy*

The heroes are those who find joy within themselves.

OCTOBER 11 – *The healing power of motherhood*

The essence of motherhood is not restricted to women who have given birth; it is a principle inherent in both women and men. It is the attitude of the mind. It is love – and that love is the very breath of life. No one would say, 'I will breathe only when I am with my family and friends; I won't breathe in front of my enemies.' Similarly, for those in whom motherhood has awakened, love and compassion towards everyone are as much part of their being as breathing. Amma feels that the forthcoming age should be dedicated to reawakening the healing power of motherhood.

OCTOBER 12 – *Free yourself from dependency*

Mind alone is the cause of all bondage and freedom. Spirituality is that principle which releases the mind from diverse thoughts and emotions, and from its dependence on external objects. It helps the mind to reach the state of eternal freedom and independence. It is the attitude of 'I' and 'mine' which makes us dependent. Practising the spiritual principles is the path that will lead us to liberation.

OCTOBER 13 – *Nothing is insignificant*

In India, we have a long tradition of respecting and revering Nature and all living beings. Our ancestors built shrines to, and worshiped, trees, birds and even poisonous snakes. A honeybee may be tiny, but without this tiny creature, pollination would cease and entire species could become extinct. If a plane's engine breaks down, the plane will not be able to fly. In fact, the absence of just one vital screw can have the same effect. Can we throw away the screw, saying that – unlike the engine – it's just a small, insignificant thing? In truth, everything has its own function and importance. Nothing is insignificant.

OCTOBER 14 – *Becoming aware of the True Self*

Whether we are aware of it or not, the real purpose of life is to realize the divinity within. There are many things you may not know in your present mental state. It is childish to say, 'They are non-existent, because I am not aware of them.' As situations and experiences unfold, new and unknown phases of life will open up, which will take you closer and closer to your own True Self. It is only a question of time. For some, this realization may have already occurred; for certain others, it will happen any moment; and yet there are others who will realize it at a later stage. Just because it has not happened yet or may not even happen in this lifetime, don't think that it is never going to happen.

Within you, immense knowledge is waiting for your permission to unfold. But it won't happen unless you allow it to.

OCTOBER 15 – *Worship Nature*

In the old days, there was no specific need for environmental preservation because protecting Nature was part of worshiping God and life itself. More than remembering God, people used to love and serve Nature and society. They saw the Creator through the creation. They loved, worshiped and protected Nature as the visible form of God. Let us try to reawaken this attitude. At present the biggest threat to mankind is not a third world war, but the loss of Nature's harmony and our widening separation from Nature.

OCTOBER 16 – *Accepting help*

To receive help, first accept that you are a patient and then be patient.

OCTOBER 17 – *Follow the scriptures*

If there is a wound on your body, you don't just sit and cry – you apply some medicine and dress the wound, otherwise it may become infected and make you weak. When you understand the essence of spiritual life, you won't be weakened by trivial things. The way to avoid sorrow is to keep the mind on the Self.

It is true that the mind cannot easily be brought under control, nor can it be done in an instant. It is difficult to cross the ocean, but those who make the effort and learn the method are able to get across.

The sages have told us the way to cross this ocean of existence. The scriptures are the instructions they have given us. We only have to follow them.

OCTOBER 18 - *Prayer - a powerful step towards God*

Is there any religion in which devotion and prayer do not have a place? You will find both devotion and prayer in Buddhism, Christianity and Islam.

All these religions also have the master–disciple relationship.

Through our prayers we are trying to imbibe divine qualities; we are trying to realize the Absolute. Prayer is not a way of weakness – it is a powerful step towards God.

OCTOBER 19 - *No more than necessary*

Amma isn't saying that you don't need wealth or worldly objects. Let there be enough of that to meet your needs in life, but not more. Be aware of what is everlasting and gives you peace, and strive to gain that. Heaven and hell exist here on earth. It is the mind that creates either heaven or hell. So, the mind needs to be controlled. Then we won't have to experience sorrow. There will be only bliss, bliss and bliss.

OCTOBER 20 – *'I am love'*

My children, we don't realize the truth that we are in bondage because of our attachment to our relationships. Not that we shouldn't have relationships, but when we develop attachments, we should clearly be aware of the place we give that object or person in our life. Only when the relationship is one of mutual understanding will true love develop. Whether the attachment is to a person or to an object, it shouldn't grow or weaken according to the circumstances. People say 'I love you!' but those are not the right words. 'I am love, the very embodiment of love' – this is the truth. When we say 'I love you' there is an 'I' and a 'you'. And love gets squeezed somewhere in between. What flows from us to others should be love and nothing but love. Love shouldn't increase or decrease according to the circumstances.

OCTOBER 21 – *Discovering our special ability*

No two blades of grass, no two flower petals are the same. What then to say of human beings? God has sent each person to earth with a special hidden ability. Each of our births has a purpose that only we can fulfil. Discovering that special power within us is the purpose of our life. That is when life becomes meaningful – a joyous communion.

OCTOBER 22 – *Beyond intellect*

We may deny God, but the intellect can neither prove nor disprove God. If the intellect were able to prove God's existence, it would only mean that the intellect is greater than God. If God could be understood through the intellect, then God and religion wouldn't be necessary at all. Science and the intellect would be enough. A God under the control of the intellect is not what we need. What we need is faith in a Supreme Power that controls the entire universe and that is beyond the mind and senses. We should inquire into the very source of that Power, which exists within ourselves. Faith in that Cosmic Power, together with meditation to know that Supreme Power, will help us attain knowledge of the Self, unity, peace and tranquility.

OCTOBER 23 – *Rebirth*

A woman was once given a beautiful crystal chandelier as first prize in an art competition. She hung it in her drawing room. While enjoying its beauty, she observed that some of the paint on the wall had begun to crumble. She decided to paint the whole room. When she had finished painting, she looked at the room and noticed that a curtain was dirty. She immediately washed all the curtains. Then it came to her attention that the old rug on the floor had become threadbare. So she removed the rug and replaced it with a new one. Finally, the room looked like new. It all began with her hanging the new lamp in the room, and ended up with the room becoming clean and beautiful, having undergone a complete transformation. Similarly, if you begin to do one good thing in life regularly, many good things will follow naturally in its wake – it will be like a rebirth. This is the only way in which a transformation is possible.

OCTOBER 24 – *Understanding rites*

There was a man who performed puja, ritual worship every day, in his family temple. One day, he got everything ready, and as he began the worship, his cat came in and drank the milk meant for the offering. The next day, as he got ready for the ceremony, he placed the cat under a basket. Only after the puja was over did he set the cat free. He made it a practice to put the cat under a basket every day before he started. The years went by in this way. When he died, his son took over the family puja. He continued the ritual of putting a basket over the cat. One day, he got everything ready for the puja and looked for the cat. The cat could not be found. He discovered that the cat had died. He didn't waste any time. He brought a cat from his neighbours' and put it under a basket, and only then did he proceed with the ritual!

The son never asked why the cat was placed under the basket. He simply followed his father's practice, without looking for the reason behind it. Today, most people observe rituals in the same way. They never try to learn the principles behind them; they just repeat what others have done before them.

Whatever our religion may be, we should try to learn the principles behind the different rituals. This is what needs to be done now. If we do this, any rituals that are meaningless will not survive.

OCTOBER 25 – *Open your eyes*

In today's world, what is most important is often not accepted, being declared as 'impractical'. This is one of the characteristics of the Kaliyuga, the age of materialistic darkness. It is easy to awaken a person who is sleeping, but difficult to awaken somebody who is pretending to be asleep. Is there any use of holding a mirror in front of a blind person? In this age, people prefer to keep their eyes closed to Truth.

OCTOBER 26 – *The need for spiritual practice*

If we wish to reach the goal, it is our duty to follow the path as it has been set out in the scriptures, and to observe the required discipline and spiritual practices. We need to develop the necessary humility to bow down before every single thing.

Nowadays, it is the ego that rules. When the grain grows into a rice plant, the plant automatically bends down. As it matures, the coconut bunch bows down from the palm tree. These examples teach us that when we develop perfect wisdom, we naturally become humble.

We can compare studying the scriptures with building a wall around an orchard, while spiritual practices represent the act of growing and tending the fruit trees within the orchard walls. The wall protects the trees, but to obtain fruit, you have to plant the trees and tend to them. Spiritual practices are absolutely necessary.

OCTOBER 27 – *Happiness does not depend on the material*

Mother is not in any way criticizing or belittling scientific discoveries, but they shouldn't dry up the wellspring of love within us. We have improved the external world, but the inner world is withering away. In the past, people received the training they needed to keep their minds under control in all circumstances. They didn't have to go through life weakened by insignificant things. If you fall into deep water, you won't survive if you don't know how to swim, regardless of what else you may have learned. Likewise, however much you increase your material comforts, you cannot enjoy peace of mind without having trained your mind. In the future, people will become very weak if they are unable to find repose within themselves, because increasingly there won't be anyone who loves them selflessly. Courageous are those who find peace within their own minds.

OCTOBER 28 – *Only the present moment is important*

Brooding over the past is like hugging a corpse! People who are dead will never come back to us. The time that has gone by will not return. Similarly, it is useless to think about what may happen in the future, for that too is just a dream. It may or may not happen. Only this moment is useful.

OCTOBER 29 – *And so we forgive*

Suppose you accidentally poke your eye with one of your hands. Your other hand doesn't slap the hand that hurt the eye, does it? There's no question of punishment. You simply forgive your hand. If your foot is hurt by accidentally stumbling into something, or if you cut your hand, you just bear it. You are ever so patient with your eyes, hands and feet, because you know they are part of your own body. No matter how much pain they may cause you from time to time, you bear it. In the same way, we should look upon others as being part of ourselves.

We should have the understanding: 'I am the cause of everything. I am in everything. No one is separate from me.' Then we won't look at the mistakes of others; and even if we do see their mistakes, we treat those errors as our own and we forgive them.

OCTOBER 30 – *Taste the sweetness*

No matter how much sugar you eat, you can't explain exactly how sweet it is to those who have never tasted sugar. Nor can words describe the infinite sky. Spirituality is beyond words – it is an experience. You cannot savour its sweetness without going beyond the intellect to the heart.

OCTOBER 31 – *Say yes to life*

Only when you see life as it truly is, and all the precious gifts it offers you, will you be able to say yes to it.

NOVEMBER

NOVEMBER 1 – *The mirage of image*

There was a disciple who didn't like giving alms. His spiritual master knew this and went to his house, disguised as a beggar. He arrived as the disciple was busy offering milk and fruits in front of a picture of the master. The master begged for some food, but the disciple drove him away, shouting, 'There's nothing here for you!' The master then removed his disguise. The disciple was devastated and prostrated at the master's feet.

We are all like that disciple. We love only the external. We don't love the inner essence. We make offerings to a picture, but give not even a penny to the beggar!

NOVEMBER 2 – *Ash and dust*

At the cremation grounds, all material desires and the body which is used to fulfil those desires are reduced to ashes. And there, where those desires are absent and there is no body consciousness, Lord Shiva dances in bliss. That's why he is called the resident of the cremation grounds. The meaning of this is not that bliss comes to us only after death. Everything is within us. We and the universe are one. Both are equally complete. When the attachment to the body dies in the fire of Self-awareness, we are automatically filled with bliss.

Shiva's body is decorated with the ashes of the funeral pyres. This is the symbol of having conquered all desires. Furthermore, the mind becomes aware of the perishable nature of the body. This inspires us to remember that this body will soon perish and that we should do good deeds as soon as possible, before the body dies.

Detachment means not giving undue importance to name or position, bodily comfort, family or friends. If we don't develop real detachment, our happiness will depend on the tip of other people's tongues! Our life will turn into a puppet in the hands of others.

Dispassion is what gives us true freedom. If we have dispassion, nothing in the world can conceal the bliss that is innate in us. Shiva, who wears ashes and resides in the funeral pyres, teaches us this principle. This is why Lord Shiva is considered the first among gurus.

NOVEMBER 3 – *Living in the light*

To turn one's back on people, claiming that there is only evil everywhere – that is the way of the lazy. If, instead of talking about the evil of others, we were to do all we could to awaken the goodness within ourselves, only then we could give light to others. This is the easiest way to change ourselves – and society as well – for the better.

Instead of blaming the encircling darkness, light your own little candle. Don't feel daunted at the thought of trying to dispel the darkness of the world with the small light within you. If you simply light your candle and move forward, it will shine its light at every step of your way, and will benefit those around you.

NOVEMBER 4 – *Breaking down our resistance*

As long as the ego remains, we cannot become selfless. The spiritual master leads the disciple through situations that are necessary to remove the ego. The disciple learns to chisel away the ego. Because of the disciple's proximity to the master and the counsel he receives from the master, the disciple develops patience without even being aware of it. The master puts the disciple in situations in which his patience is tested and his anger may arise. The disciple is given the type of work he doesn't like. This will make the disciple angry and he will disobey. Then the master will encourage the disciple to reflect. The disciple will find within himself the strength needed to transcend difficult situations. Thus the master uses different situations to eliminate the weaknesses of the disciple and to make him strong. This enables the disciple to transcend the ego. It is for the purpose of eliminating the ego that we take refuge in a master.

Only when a conch shell is emptied of the flesh that was inside it can any sound come out of it when it is blown. Similarly, when we become free of the ego, we can rise to our spiritual goal. Once complete surrender has taken place, there is no longer any sense of 'I' – there is only God.

NOVEMBER 5 – *Choose the right path*

Happiness and sorrow depend on our minds, not on external things. Heaven and hell exist here on earth. If we understand the proper place of each material object in our lives and live accordingly, there will be no cause for grief. The knowledge which teaches us how to live on this earth, how to live a contented life in the face of all obstacles, is spiritual knowledge, knowledge about mastering the mind. This is what we need to acquire first of all. Once we are aware of the good and bad side of things, we can choose the path that leads to everlasting joy.

NOVEMBER 6 – *That which never dies*

Whatever will perish is not real. All the forms, even of the gods and goddesses have a beginning and an end. That which is born and dies is mental; it is associated with the thought process. And whatever is associated with the mind is bound to change, because it exists in time. The only unchangeable truth is that which always remains – the substratum of the mind and intellect. That is the Atman [Self], the ultimate state of existence.

NOVEMBER 7 – *Omnipresent Universal Consciousness*

There is no need to search for a God sitting somewhere beyond the sky. God is the all-pervading Universal Consciousness. Still, we advise people to meditate on a form, because a medium is necessary to make the mind one-pointed. To construct a slab of concrete, we first have to make a wooden frame, and it is into that frame that we pour the concrete. When the concrete has set, we can remove the frame. This can be compared to worshiping a divine form. The form is required in the beginning until the principles are firmly grasped. Once the mind is firmly established in the Universal Self, there is no longer any need for any such tools.

NOVEMBER 8 – *Expressing emotions*

Enlightenment is not a rock-like state where one loses all inner feelings. It is a state of mind, a spiritual attainment into which you can withdraw yourself and remain absorbed whenever you want. After you tap into the infinite source of energy, your capacity to feel and express everything gains a special, unearthly beauty and depth. If an enlightened person wishes, he or she can express emotions in whichever intensity he or she desires.

Sri Rama cried when the demon king Ravana kidnapped his consort, Sita. In fact, lamenting like any ordinary human being, he asked everyone in the forest, 'Have you seen my Sita? Where did she go, leaving me alone?' Krishna's eyes were filled with tears when he saw his friend Sudama after a very long time. Similar incidents are there in Christ's and Buddha's lives as well. These mahatmas were as expansive as limitless space and therefore could reflect any emotion they wanted. They were reflective, not reactive.

Like a mirror, mahatmas respond to situations with perfect spontaneity. Eating when you are hungry is a response. Whereas eating whenever you see food is a reaction. It is also a disease. Responding to a particular situation, remaining unaffected by it and then moving on to the next moment is what a mahatma does.

Feeling emotions and honestly sharing them without reservation only adds to an enlightened being's spiritual splendour and glory. It is wrong to see that as a weakness. It should rather be considered as an expression of their compassion and love in a much more human way.

NOVEMBER 9 – *Love until you become one*

Real love has nothing to do with lust or self-centredness. In real love, you are not important; the other is important. In love, the other is not your instrument to fulfil your selfish desires; you are an instrument of the Divine with the intention of doing good in the world. Love does not sacrifice others; love gives joyfully of itself. Love is selfless. In real love, you do not feel worthless; on the contrary, you expand and become one with everything – all encompassing, ever blissful.

NOVEMBER 10 – *The essential*

Selfless service, renunciation, surrender and compassion are all essential.

NOVEMBER 11 – *The purifying virtue of patience*

In every stone exists a latent image. When the sculptor chisels away all the unwanted parts, the image emerges. That beautiful form is born because

the stone offers itself to the artist, sitting patiently
before him or her for a long time.

A stone lying at the bottom of the Sabarimala
Mountain (an important pilgrimage centre in India)
complains to the image of the Lord that is worshiped
in the temple, 'You are a stone just like me, and yet
you are worshiped by everyone, while I am being
trampled. What justice is this?' The image replies:
'Now you see only that everyone worships me. But
before I came here, a sculptor chiselled away at me
hundreds of thousands of times. During all that
time, I lay patiently before the sculptor, without the
slightest resistance. As a result of this, I am here now
and am being worshiped by millions.' The patience of
the stone has transformed it into an image of worship.

NOVEMBER 12 - *The One in the many*

The more subtle and expansive the mind becomes,
the more it becomes 'no-mind'. Gradually, the mind
disappears. When there is no mind, where is God
and where is the world or creation? Nevertheless,
this doesn't mean that the world will disappear from
your sight, it means a transformation will happen
and you will behold the One in the many.

NOVEMBER 13 - *Love is the ultimate religion*

Indeed love is the only religion that can help
humanity rise to great and glorious heights. And

love should be the one thread on which are strung all the religions and philosophies of the world. The beauty of society lies in the unity of hearts.

NOVEMBER 14 – *Put down your burdens*

My children, we may carry many burdens of sorrow – the son hasn't found a job, the daughter isn't married, we haven't built the house we dreamed of, we don't get cured of our illness, there is family discord, the business is running at a loss, and so on. We burn like rice husks, thinking about all our troubles. The mind is tense, and this tension is the cause of all diseases.

The only way to remove this tension is to surrender. What is the use of undergoing all that stress and suffering? We need to perform our actions to the best of our ability, using the strength that God has given us, and then let things unfold according to God's will. Leave everything to the Supreme Being. Taking total refuge in God is the only way. There's no use in letting yourself burn, thinking about what is gone and what is yet to come. Only this present moment is with you. Be careful not to lose this moment because of your sorrow.

NOVEMBER 15 – *Don't pontificate*

The older generation should employ the approach of dialogue. When approaching young people, we shouldn't try to demonstrate our own knowledge and erudition. We should become one with them, understand their hearts and engage them in discussions. We should patiently listen to their questions and criticism. We should approach them with compassion. Only such an approach will create real change within them. Above all else, we should give them examples that will inspire them.

NOVEMBER 16 – *Meditate!*

Meditation increases your vitality and strengthens your intelligence; your beauty is enhanced and your mental clarity and health improve. You acquire the patience and fortitude to face the problems in life. So meditate. Through meditation you will find the treasure you are looking for.

NOVEMBER 17 – *There is only love*

Amma's connection with Nature is not a relationship; it is total Oneness. A lover of God is a lover of Nature as well, because God and Nature are not two. Once you attain the state of enlightenment, you become connected to the whole universe. In Amma's relationship with Nature, there is no lover or beloved – love alone is. There are not two; there is only one; there is only love.

NOVEMBER 18 – *Neither 'me' nor 'mine'*

Seeing God in all things, perceiving everything as one and the same, knowing all beings as your own Self – that is realization. When all thoughts have subsided and there are no more desires, when the mind is perfectly still, only then you experience a state in which the attitude of 'I' and 'mine' has vanished. You are then of service to everyone, and no longer a burden to others. An ordinary person can be compared to a small, stagnant pond, while a realized soul is like a river, or a tree, giving comfort and coolness to those who come to him.

NOVEMBER 19 – *The tree of life*

In the soil of love, let good deeds be the leaves on the tree, may words of kindness form its flowers and may peace be its fruit.

NOVEMBER 20 – *Intense longing*

Say you are now standing at the foot of a mountain. Before even beginning the ascent, you must first give up your attachment to the valley and everything you possess. If you do not do this with all your heart, you will undoubtedly suffer. Otherwise, there is no suffering. When you have renounced this attachment, the suffering becomes an intense longing, the longing to reach the summits of eternal union. The true question is: 'How many are willing to give up this attachment with all their heart?'

NOVEMBER 21 - *Temple rituals*

The temple is a place where the remembrance of God is kindled, at least for a short while, even for those who are otherwise immersed in worldliness. However, we shouldn't stay bound to temple rituals until the end of our lives. Nothing bad can happen to us if we practise prayer and meditation every day in solitude without visiting a temple. If we do not establish God firmly in our heart, even a lifetime of temple worship will do us no good.

NOVEMBER 22 - *No attachment, no aversion*

View everything you come across with discrimination and awareness. Do not harbour any feelings of attachment or aversion towards anything. Then, everything will have something to teach you. We have to transform our way of seeing in order to perceive the light of knowledge. The attitude of being a disciple, the attitude of surrender, helps you to achieve this.

NOVEMBER 23 - *Wipe the tears of the ones who suffer*

There is no end to the war and death caused by man or to the tears shed by all the innocent victims of such tragedies. What are all these tragedies for?

Only for conquering, establishing superiority and satisfying our greed for money and fame. Mankind has taken upon itself countless curses. In order to attain freedom from these curses, at least a hundred generations to come should wipe the tears of the suffering, striving to console them and alleviate their pain.

NOVEMBER 24 – *Pray, then eat*

Not a grain of the food we eat is made purely by our own effort. What comes to us in the form of food is the toil of our fellow men, the bounty of nature, and God's compassion. Even if we have millions of dollars, we still need food to satisfy our hunger. After all, we cannot eat dollars. So we should never eat anything without first praying with humility and gratitude.

NOVEMBER 25 – *Master our thoughts*

Our thoughts are our own creation. We make them real by cooperating with them. If we remove our support from them, they just dissolve. Look closely at your thoughts without judging them and see how they gradually fade.

NOVEMBER 26 – *The flow of life*

A drop of water cannot be a river; a river is formed by numerous water drops. It is the joining together of countless drops that creates a flow. The real flow of life lies in unity, in the oneness that arises out of love.

NOVEMBER 27 – *Anger is a poison*

Children, you won't really benefit from your spiritual practices if you do them while at the same time harbouring anger and pride. It is like putting sugar on one side and ants on the other: the ants will eat all the sugar. And you're not even noticing what's happening! Whatever you have gained by your sadhana, you lose through your anger. A flashlight running on batteries loses all its power after you have turned it on a number of times, doesn't it? In the same way, whenever you get angry, you lose your energy through your eyes, nose, mouth, ears and through every pore of your body. Only by practising mental restraint can you preserve the energy you have gained from your practice.

NOVEMBER 28 – *True happiness*

God is the personification of compassion, standing humbly with both arms extended towards us to receive our ego. The ego is what God likes the most as an offering from us, and that is what we should offer to God. If we are not ready to do this, God will somehow extract the ego from us! God knows that only when this is done can we experience true happiness. This surrender to the Supreme Spirit brings about the purification of the mind and intellect. This is how we can transform life into a festival.

November 29 - *Consciousness engenders respect*

Everything is pervaded by Divine Consciousness. It is that Consciousness which sustains the world and all the creatures in it. To worship everything, seeing God in all is what religion advises. Such an attitude teaches us to love Nature. None of us would consciously injure our own body because we know it would be painful. Similarly, we will feel the pain of other people to be our own when the realization dawns within us that everything is pervaded by one and the same Consciousness. Compassion will arise and we will sincerely wish to help and protect all. In that state, we won't feel like plucking even a leaf unnecessarily. We will pick a flower only on the last day of its existence, just before it falls from the stem. We will consider it as very harmful to the plant and to Nature if the flower is picked on its very first day, due to our greediness.

November 30 - *Supreme detachment*

There was a mahatma whose only job was to roll big boulders up to the top of a mountain. That was

the only work he did until his death. He never got
bored or had any complaints. Sometimes it would
take several hours or even days to single-handedly
roll a boulder all the way to the top of the mountain.
And once he managed to get it there, he would roll
it down. Looking at the boulder rolling down from
the top to the foot of the mountain, he would clap
his hands and burst into laughter like a small child.

Ascension in any field of action takes a lot
of courage and energy, but it doesn't even take
a moment to destroy everything that we have
acquired through hard work. This is very true even
about virtues.

Also this great soul was not at all attached to
all the sincere effort that he had put forth to roll
this boulder uphill. This is why he could laugh
like a child – the laughter of supreme detachment.
Probably these are the lessons he wished to teach
everyone.

DECEMBER

December 1 – *From the head to the heart*

This is the age of intellect and reason, the age of
science. We have forgotten the feelings of the
heart. A common expression the world over is 'I
have fallen in love'. Yes, we have fallen down into a
love rooted in selfishness and materialism. We are
unable to arise and awaken in Love. If fall we must,
let it be from the head to the heart.

December 2 – *Embrace life*

Most people are frightened when they hear of
spirituality. Spirituality doesn't mean that you
shouldn't acquire any wealth or that you should
give up family life. You can become wealthy and
lead a family life, but your life should be based
on an understanding of the spiritual principles.
Family life and the acquisition of wealth, without

171

any awareness of the spiritual principles, is like collecting combs for a bald head! Our wealth and our relationship with our family are not going to be with us always. We should therefore accord them only the place they deserve in life.

By understanding spirituality, we can embrace the world even more joyfully. Spirituality teaches us how to gain the courage and strength to enjoy bliss in this life itself.

DECEMBER 3 – *Transcend religious conditioning*

In fact, religion is a constraint created by humans. At birth we had no conditioning or limitations regarding religion or language. These have been taught to us, conditioning us over time. Just as a small plant needs a fence, this conditioning is necessary to a certain extent. Once the seedling grows into a tree, it transcends the fence. Similarly, we must be able to go beyond our religious conditioning and become 'unconditional'.

DECEMBER 4 – *Respond to hate with love*

When there is a difference of opinion, be ready to discuss the matter and resolve the problem that same day, instead of postponing it. Anyone can return love for love – there is nothing great in that. Try also to return love for hatred. This alone is the true measure of our greatness. Only when we are able to forgive others and accept their faults and shortcomings will peace prevail in society.

DECEMBER 5 – *Remove the veil that obscures our divinity*

Say that a 100-watt light bulb hangs in the kitchen. The bulb is so covered by soot that it doesn't even give the output of a 10-watt bulb. If we wipe off the soot, the bulb will once again shine with its full brilliance. Similarly, spiritual practice is the process of removing our impurities. By removing the veil that obscures our innate divinity, we will experience the infinite power within us. We will understand that we weren't born to experience sorrow, but that our true nature is bliss. However, it is not enough to simply talk about these truths. Spiritual practice is required. Everyone has the innate capacity to swim, but only if we get into the water and practise, will we learn how to swim. Devotion and prayer are means by which we awaken the Divinity within us.

DECEMBER 6 – *Don't miss the goal*

Religion points the way like a road sign. The goal is spiritual experience.

DECEMBER 7 – *Faith and experience*

God is all-pervading, but His presence can be felt more easily by those who have faith in the temple.

But for this to happen, faith is essential. Faith tunes the mind. Even though God is present in the temple, those who lack faith won't experience that feeling. It is faith that gives us the experience.

DECEMBER 8 – *Awaken the child in us*

My children, not one of you is an ordinary person! Each of you possesses extraordinary powers. There is infinite strength within us, but it's sleeping at the moment. We just have to awaken it. Then, victory is certain.

Our bodies have grown, but our minds haven't. For our minds to grow as large as the universe, we have to become like children. We have to awaken the child within us. Only a child can grow. What we have within us today is the ego, and nothing can be gained with that sense of 'I'. It has to disappear, and a sense of expansiveness has to take its place.

DECEMBER 9 – *Awareness and gratitude*

No matter what you are busy doing after the archana [worship], always try to keep the thought of God alive.

Whenever you sit down or stand up, do so after bowing down to the ground. It is good to cultivate the habit of thinking that your pen, books, clothes, vessels and work tools are imbued with the Divine Presence, and to consequently use everything with care and respect. This will help you maintain a constant remembrance of God.

DECEMBER 10 – *Relieve suffering*

Real prayer includes being compassionate and humble towards others, smiling at someone and saying a kind word. We should learn to forgive the mistakes of others and to be deeply compassionate – just as our one hand automatically caresses the other hand if it is in pain. By developing love, understanding and broad-mindedness, we can ease the pain of so many people.

DECEMBER 11 – *Pray in happiness and in pain*

Children, the tears that flow when one prays to God with love are not tears of sorrow; they are tears of bliss. Nowadays, people pray to God only during times of distress. If you pray to God in times of both happiness and sadness, you will no longer have to experience any suffering. Even if some suffering should come to you, it won't appear as suffering.

God will look after you. If you can pray to Him with an open heart and shed a few tears out of love for Him, you are saved.

DECEMBER 12 – *Universal love*

When Amma embraces people it is not just physical contact that is taking place. The love Amma feels for all of creation flows towards each person who comes to Her. That pure vibration of love purifies people and helps them in their inner awakening and spiritual growth.

Both men and women of today's world need to awaken to motherly qualities. Amma's hugs are to help people become aware of this universal need.

Love is the only language that every living being can understand. It is universal.

DECEMBER 13 – *Make room*

God will appear only when all views disappear.

DECEMBER 14 – *Perfect freedom*

Human beings are slaves to their thoughts. The pressure created by these thoughts makes you a helpless victim to outside situations. There are countless thoughts and emotions, both subtle and gross in a person. Unable to look closely and discriminate between good ones and bad ones, between the productive and destructive, people easily fall prey to harmful impulses and become identified with negative emotions. In the supreme state of sannyas, one has the choice between identifying with or being detached from each particular emotion and thought. You have the choice to cooperate or not to cooperate with each thought, emotion and given situation. Even if you choose to cooperate, you have the option to withdraw at any time you want. This indeed is complete freedom.

DECEMBER 15 – *The heart is a temple*

Your heart is the temple, and that is where God should be installed. Good thoughts are the flowers that you offer Him, good deeds are the worship, kind words are the hymns, and love is the sacred food offering.

DECEMBER 16 – *Taken to task*

When a superior takes you to task, think of it as an opportunity provided by God to help work your ego, and dismiss any hostile feeling that may arise within you. Similarly, if you have to deal sternly with a subordinate, take care not to let any anger or resentment arise within you. In the eyes of a true spiritual aspirant, superiors, subordinates and colleagues are all different forms of God.

DECEMBER 17 – *The power of prayer*

Prayer is not a weakness. If we pray with faith and sincerity, we can awaken the love that lies dormant within us.

DECEMBER 18 – *Love. Do not blame.*

Expecting men to change immediately is unreasonable. They are being led by a mind that is unknown to them. If someone falls in front of an elephant, the elephant will raise its leg to step on him. Even a baby elephant will do that. Such is the power of ingrained nature. Instead of blaming men, we should patiently and lovingly strive to change them.

DECEMBER 19 – *Learn from past mistakes*

It is pointless to brood over the past. The past is like a cancelled check – no longer valid. In order to create a positive future, given all the pain and destruction that have been inflicted in the past, we have to be willing to forgive; this is fundamental to all religions. Yet, we must learn from the past, or we will repeat our mistakes. After a thorn pricks our foot, we become alert with each step; this alertness could be what saves us from falling into a dangerous pit further on. It is from this perspective that we should view the painful experiences from the past. Those who have harmed others in the past should now engage in positive actions to uplift the victims of their past oppression. These principles apply to governments as well as to individuals. In order to heal the wounds, broken relationships should be stitched with the thread of love. For this to be possible, more than intellectual knowledge, we should have an awareness of oneness.

DECEMBER 20 – *Do not take love for attachment*

'Am I really in love or am I too attached?' Ask yourself this question as deeply as you can. Contemplate this. And soon you will realize that the love we know is really attachment. Most people are craving attachment, not real love. So Amma would say this is an illusion. In a way, we are betraying ourselves. We mistake attachment for love. Love is the centre and attachment is in the periphery. Be in the centre and detach yourself from the periphery. Then the pain will go away.

DECEMBER 21 – *God's dearest dwelling place*

A kind heart is enough – that is the first step on the spiritual path. A person who does this need not go anywhere in search of God. God will come running to the heart that is full of compassion. That is God's dearest dwelling place.

DECEMBER 22 – *Kindness*

My children, do not look at the faults and failures of others, and do not talk about such things. Always try to see only the good in everyone. We should serve others with kindness, without blaming anyone for their faults.

DECEMBER 23 – *Have faith in the words of the masters*

Don't we believe the scientists when they talk of the Moon and Mars? Yet how many of us can really confirm that what they say is true? Still we trust the words of the scientists and the astronomers, don't we? Likewise, the saints and seers of the past performed years of experiments in their inner laboratories and realized the Supreme Truth, which is the substratum of the universe. Just as we trust the words of the scientists who talk about facts unknown to us, we should have faith in the words of the great masters who speak about the Truth, in which they are established.

DECEMBER 24 – *See others as yourself*

In order to consider others – nature or human beings – the first and foremost quality that one needs to develop is a deep inner connection, a connection with one's own conscience. Conscience, in the real sense, is the power to see others as yourself. Just as you see your own image in a mirror, you see others as you. You reflect others, their feelings, both happiness and sorrow. We have to develop this capacity in our relationships with nature and our fellow beings.

December 25 – *Discernment and an open heart*

The heart and the intellect are not two separate things. When you have a discriminating intellect, you will naturally become expansive. From that expansiveness, a spirit of innocence, compromise, humbleness and a willingness to help others will naturally arise. The word *heart* stands for that expansiveness. Even at the very mention of the word *heart*, we feel a soothing gentleness.

The ego is the cause of all the suffering in life. As the ego grows, the person's expansiveness contracts, and the spirit of compromise disappears. One cannot do without these qualities, either in spiritual life or in worldly life.

December 26 – *Living our spirituality*

Spirituality isn't something to be just talked about; it has to be lived.

December 27 – *The true nature of the world*

If you wish to experience peace without end, you need to have an understanding of what is everlasting and what is fleeting. A pet snake is given milk even though it could bite. But we should remember that it is a snake we are feeding, because it is bound to show its true nature. If we understand people's true nature when we are dealing with them, we won't end up being disappointed. As we deal with the world, we should be aware of its true nature.

DECEMBER 28 – *Letting go*

We should be attached to the world while keeping a detached attitude. Attach and detach at will; act, then let go and continue … act again, then let go and continue on your way. The superfluous luggage of dreams, desires and attachment make the journey of our lives extremely unhappy.

DECEMBER 29 – *Spiritual practice is a vital necessity*

Spirituality should not be a part-time occupation. It is a full-time job. Amma does not ask you to leave your job nor to work less. You consider your work and earning money as serious business, don't you? Well, realizing God is also serious business. Spiritual practices should be a part of your everyday life, just as eating and sleeping are.

DECEMBER 30 – *Pray for peace in the world*

Amma is not going to trouble you with more words. My children, close your eyes and pray for world peace. Pray sincerely that you will be given the selfless heart of a mother.

DECEMBER 31 – *May all beings ...*

Let us pray and meditate together. That is the best way to reach the shore of peace. When we meditate and pray as a group, the life energy of all of us will harmoniously flow to a single stream spreading a divine fragrance soaked in the sweetness of love.

This will create vibrations of peace and unity in the atmosphere. Attuning our minds with the one Supreme Power and forgetting all thoughts of division, let us open our hearts and sincerely utter the following prayer:

May all beings in this world and in all the other worlds be peaceful and happy.

ACKNOWLEDGEMENTS

Editions Points and the 'Points Vivre' collection extend their most heartfelt thanks to Brahmacharini Dipamrita (Claudine Tourdes), president of ETW France and director of the Amma centre near Chartres. Performing a balancing act with her demanding schedule, she helped us every step of the way in this project, no matter where she happened to be in the world. We are deeply grateful for her trust, her delicate and enlightened guidance, and for the joyful radiance she brought to each of our meetings.

We would also like to thank M.A. Math for the translation of this book into English, and especially Annie Delemotte and Geni Lawrence of ETW France, who worked with professionalism and commitment. Their teamwork is a living example of Amma's teachings.